Mary Bohlen's
HERITAGE COOKING

MERCER UNIVERSITY PRESS

Endowed by
Tom Watson Brown
and
The Watson-Brown Foundation, Inc.

MUP/ P603

Published by Mercer University Press
1501 Mercer University Drive
Macon, Georgia 31207

9 8 7 6 5 4 3 2 1

Books published by Mercer University Press are printed on acid-free paper
that meets the requirements of the American National Standard for Information
Sciences—Permanence of Paper for Printed Library Materials.

Printed and bound in the United States.

This book is set in Caslon and Worcester Round
with titles in Archive Penman Script.

Cover and book interior designed by Burt&Burt

ISBN   978-0-88146-7383

Cataloging-in-Publication Data is available from the Library of Congress

Mary Bohlen's

HERITAGE COOKING

Inspired by

REBECCA BOONE

"This series explores the central and profound role
that food and foodways play in understanding the South's past,
its present, and its future. Through a broad variety of academic disciplines,
the series examines the region's culinary history, celebrates the glories
of the Southern table, and analyzes the many influences that
come together to define Southern food."

—Fred W. Sauceman, Series Editor

IN THE SERIES

The Proffitts of Ridgewood: An Appalachian Family's Life in Barbecue
Fred W. Sauceman

Cook & Tell: Recipes and Stories from Southern Kitchens
Johnathon Scott Barrett, ed.

E.M.C.

This book is dedicated to the memory of
EDITH MARIE CARTER,
who established Whippoorwill Village,
including the reconstructed Boone Cabin,
and to ELIZABETH,
a beloved colonial friend and teacher.

Contents

FOREWORD

REBECCA BOONE could plow, and she could shoot. While her husband, Daniel Boone, was away for months at a time on one of his famous "long hunts," Rebecca literally kept the home fires burning—feeding, clothing, and protecting their ten children as well as orphans the couple had adopted. Daniel Boone's role in exploring the backwoods of what would become the state of Kentucky has become part of American folklore. What Rebecca had to do in order to keep the family alive back in the colony of North Carolina is much less well known.

Mary Bohlen has changed that with this book, a tribute to Rebecca Boone and other pioneer women of the eighteenth century whose work was far less romanticized than that of their menfolk but equally vital to survival on the frontier.

Mary is well qualified to write about the subject. Not only has she done extensive scholarly work, she has felt the heat of the hearth. In the spirit of Rebecca Boone, she even pitched in to help build a log cabin, at Latta Plantation in Huntersville, North Carolina, where she regularly volunteers.

Mary's cooking demonstrations—at various North Carolina historic sites, along the Blue Ridge Parkway in North Carolina and Virginia, and in Colonial Williamsburg—bring the eighteenth century to life. One of her most enduring memories is serving hearth-baked ginger cakes on pewter plates at Whippoorwill, near Wilkes-boro, North Carolina, on the upper Yadkin River—likely the last place the Boones lived before they headed off to Kentucky.

Mary has made sweet potato custard with fresh local sweet potatoes at Matthews Cabin, at Mabry Mill, near Meadows of Dan, Virginia. She once baked peach pie in midsummer on the property where future United States President James K. Polk was born in Pineville, North Carolina. To the amazement of her guests, she cooked green pumpkin in a buttered cast-iron skillet at Snow Camp, settled by Quakers in 1749 in Alamance County, North Carolina. And since 2006, she has demonstrated campfire cooking at Surry Muster Field in Elkin, North Carolina, for the Overmountain Victory Trail Association. The event commemorates the Battle of Kings Mountain, described as the turning point of the American Revolution.

As Rebecca Boone most assuredly did, Mary Bohlen knows exactly how to render bear fat, and she can turn out a perfect corn cake. She presents these Colonial "receipts" as much as possible in their original form, affirming the honored place that the open hearth and the campfire occupied in the history of America.

Fred Sauceman,
Series Editor

Meet the Cook

MARY BOHLEN

On a sunny spring day in 1984, Mary Bohlen participated in an open-hearth cooking class at the Tullie Smith plantation house in Atlanta. After that, she realized she was hooked!

Mary had just finished a week-long internship at the Atlanta Historical Society (now the Atlanta History Center) through Agnes Scott College. In addition, she had just started working as a weekend docent at the historic house.

The Tullie Smith Kitchen Guild demonstrated cooking each day in the circa 1840 kitchen. Workers and volunteers at the site were able to purchase a plate lunch for one dollar.

Bohlen muses, "I often reflect on that first cooking experience. It led me on a path I had not even thought about. It opened up an avenue for me to express myself and my love of history."

With the guidance of the Kitchen Guild, the class produced one of the "most authentic, palatable meals" one could imagine—fried chicken, green beans, corn on the cob, spider corn bread, garden herb salad, apple-blueberry cobbler, and tea with a sprig of mint, all fresh and cooked 19th century style.

Upon returning to North Carolina, Mary became a volunteer at Latta Plantation in

Opposite: Mary at the corn crib. Tullie Smith Farmhouse. Atlanta. 1984

Huntersville. It was only fitting to be there, after all, just three years before, she had helped build the log cabin in which she was now cooking. She said, "Every demonstration gave me the opportunity to share my experience of cooking and of putting together the log cabin. I quickly learned that visitors liked to engage in living history demonstrations and that they strongly related to the smells and taste of food prepared on an open fire."

Reflecting, Bohlen said that she had always wanted to learn about what life was like for her great grandmothers. She agrees that it was a simpler, quieter life but that it was not always easy.

"There is something about doing it the old way that gives me a sense of connection to the past as well as a feeling of accomplishment."

Mary broadened her cooking experience when she joined a Revolutionary War living history organization. That, plus being in the educational profession, opened the door for doing cooking demonstrations at historic sites across North Carolina, on the Blue Ridge Parkway, and even at Colonial Williamsburg.

Mary has gathered and researched an extensive collection of 18th and 19th century receipts. *Foxfire # 1*, *Tullie's Receipts*, and *The Backcounty Housewife* are her favorite resources and although tattered and stained with use they have become old standbys that she often refers to for historic information and for inspiration.

"Studying about foodways is a great way to learn about the life of our ancestors and to do it in a tangible way. I very much enjoy researching old cookbooks and receipts. I never get tired of doing cooking demonstrations or the smiles of visitors when they gather around the fire and see and smell bread and pies fresh from the Dutch-oven. People connect with that kind experience and I think they see that it is not just a hobby for me, it is a part of who I am."

Above: Mary, as a child, sightseeing at Appomattox Court House, Virginia.
Below: The kitchen at Tullie Smith Farmhouse

REPLICA BOONE CABIN, Ferguson, NC

Rebecca Boone

FRONTIER WIFE ON THE YADKIN

Daniel Boone is noted to have once said, "A man needs three things for happiness: A good dog, a good gun, and a good wife." He had all three. His good wife was Rebecca Bryan Boone who often falls into the shadow of her legendary husband. Research materials on Rebecca pale in comparison to volumes that can be found on Daniel Boone's life and adventures. Details of Rebecca's life are sketchy and shrouded in folklore creating a curiosity that draws the imagination.

Edith Carter, a Yadkin Valley Boone enthusiast and owner of Whippoorwill Village, commented, "Rebecca was a remarkable woman and not enough is said about her. Think about the rustic living conditions, raising all those children—ten in one cabin—and taking care of the farmstead while Daniel was away on his long hunts!"

Growing up on the frontier Rebecca must have been well trained in survival skills. She knew how to shoot game, plow a field, keep a garden, and weave linen for her family. A woman's work in the backcountry was never-ending.

Rebecca Bryan was born near Winchester, Virginia, in 1739, to Joseph Bryan and Hester Hampton. After the death of Rebecca's mother, her father married Alice Linville. While Rebecca was still a child, the Bryan clan, with the exception of her father Joseph, moved south to the Carolina back country. It is plausible that Rebecca and her sister Martha traveled with their Bryan grandparents while Joseph stayed behind to settle his father's financial affairs before joining them.

Rebecca's family established a homestead on Deep Creek, a tributary of the Yadkin River, north of the Shallow Ford crossing. About the same time Daniel's father, Squire Boone, moved his family from Pennsylvania and Virginia to settle in the forks of the Yadkin near present day Mocksville. The two large Quaker families were well acquainted.

At one of the wedding festivities between the Boones and Bryans, Rebecca and Daniel saw each other for the first time. One story of their courtship reveals the patience of Rebecca. The couple attended a cherry-picking and as they sat on the grass together, nervous and fidgety, Daniel tosses his knife into the grass, maybe to tease Rebecca or to impress her. The knife pins her lovely cambric apron to the ground with a gash. Daniel watches Rebecca's reaction thinking that if she does not show a fiery outburst of temper then she was the girl for him. And so she was. He affectionately called her "my little girl."

The Bryan-Boone marriage was in August 1753; Rebecca, 17, and Daniel, 21. It was a triple wedding, Daniel told his children in later years. From all accounts the couple was very devoted to each other. For 10 years they lived in the Yadkin settlements near present day Farmington.

Daniel and Rebecca's home would have been a traditional log cabin of the frontier. While we have no hard documentation describing their dwelling, there are sources and period cabins that provide a good idea of how it may have been constructed.

A typical cabin was made of handhewn logs, cut 6–8 inches deep with 12 inches or more on their facings with dovetail or v-notches. A cabin might be 16 x 14 feet with one or two doors, facing either east or south, a loft and a large fireplace. It is unlikely it had windows but perhaps a loophole opening to shoot through and to allow in some light. All could be built using only pegs and in some cases handwrought nails in the doors. Floors may have been dirt or puncheon. Large field stones or rocks from nearby creeks or rivers served as foundation stones for the cabin and/or a base for the hearth. It would take about 4,000 split shingles to cover the roof.

In 1766 the Boones moved to the upper Yadkin in present day Wilkes County. Their permanent home on the river was on the north side of the mouth of Beaver Creek overlooking the bottom lands of the Yadkin. From there Daniel started making his long treks toward Kentucky, leaving the farm to the care of Rebecca. Success would depend upon her housewifery skills, her own labor, along with the help of the older children, and the family's resourcefulness.

On days when I cook on the hearth of the replica Boone cabin at Whippoorwill Village I think about Rebecca's life on the frontier and my mind is full of questions. Some answers can be found in historical records and documented family interviews yet others have not been answered at all, leaving things open to speculation. Here are a few things we do know:

Rebecca had long black hair and penetrating dark eyes. She was almost as tall as Daniel who was about 5'11." One writer stated she was an over-commonly sized woman. A descendant said Rebecca was "one of the hand-somest persons she ever saw." A granddaughter remembers that she was a neat and tidy housekeeper. Rebecca herself said that "folks ought to always keep their house in good order." It is doubtful that she could read or write.

A Moravian missionary, who traveled by the Boone home along the Yadkin, wrote in his journal that Rebecca seemed to be quite distraught at the long absences of her husband and that her home was a place of isolation.

Merchant records from Salisbury show that spices, flour, sugar, oats, and sewing goods were among some of the wares available. Since Daniel sold or traded his pelts and hides at market there, it is possible that he purchased some of these goods for Rebecca.

What we know about Rebecca Bryan Boone is mostly because of what has been written about her husband. That is a good thing because it gives us a picture of life for women on the frontier. It helps us understand the daunting task of a wife and mother. Immediately after her wedding Rebecca and Daniel took into their care Daniel's two young orphaned nephews. Rebecca gave birth to ten children, seven were born in North Carolina. Later in life she cared for more orphaned family children. She was brave, industrious, and aware of the precarious life she faced. She stood by her man. She knew how to handle a gun and plow, weave, sew, cook, and hold a family together against the perils of an untamed land. Rebecca Boone was indeed a remarkable woman. For me, she is a heroine of the American frontier.

Based on Mary Bohlen's article for *Yadkin Valley Living Magazine*, March/April 2011.

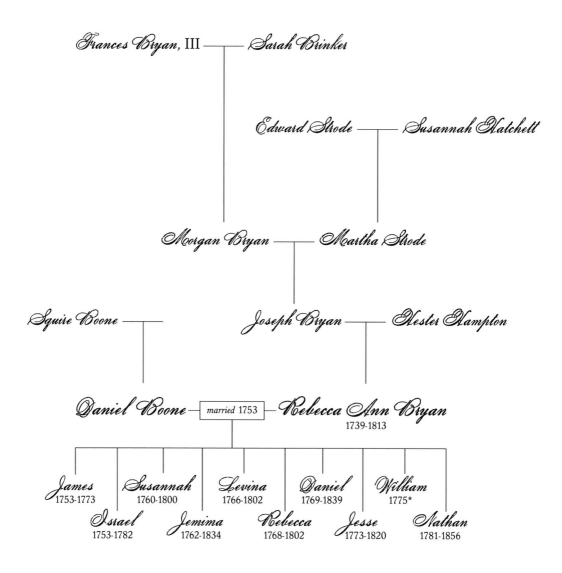

Frances Bryan, III —— Sarah Brinker

Edward Strode —— Susannah Hatchett

Morgan Bryan —— Martha Strode

Squire Boone ——   Joseph Bryan —— Hester Hampton

Daniel Boone —[married 1753]— Rebecca Ann Bryan
1739-1813

James   Susannah   Levina   Daniel   William
1753-1773   1760-1800   1766-1802   1769-1839   1775*

Israel   Jemima   Rebecca   Jesse   Nathan
1753-1782   1762-1834   1768-1802   1773-1820   1781-1856

Boone-Bryan
FAMILY TREE

*Died in infancy

THE WORLD OF
Rebecca Boone

WHO WERE THE BRYANS?

One of the most prominent families that settled on the North Carolina frontier were the Bryans. Their land assets were so large that the area became known as the "Bryan Settlements." Rebecca's grandfather, Morgan Bryan was the patriarch of this large clan and it is with him our journey begins.

The Bryan family has a rich and fascinating heritage going back to 17th century Ireland where they were landed gentry. According to tradition, the family holdings and titles were stripped by Crown officials because of political differences and for this reason, and perhaps more, Morgan's father, Francis Bryan III moved to Denmark. There he married Sarah Brinker Bryan. Morgan Bryan was born in Denmark in 1671 and lived there until his early teens when the family moved back to Ireland.

Virtually nothing is known about Morgan's early years. It is believed that he emigrated to America about 1718, eventually settling in Chester County, Pennsylvania, where he married Martha Strode Bryan.

Martha Strode Bryan, Rebecca's grandmother, was born in France about 1696. Her parents were Edward and Susannah Hatchett Strode of Somerset County, England. It is said that the Strodes fled to France because of political unrest and eventually set sail for America. Both of Martha's parents died in voyage, leaving her a orphan. Some say Martha was taken in by family or that she may have been "bound out" or indentured until she was grown.

Together, Morgan and Martha Bryan had seven sons and two daughters. Their first child was Joseph, the father of Rebecca Ann Bryan Boone.

Learning the origin of Rebecca Bryan's family is important to me. Understanding her ancestry helps in the study of foodways that might be connected to her family. What food traditions did her grandparents bring to America and were they passed down through generations of daughters? How does all this connect with the hearth and home of a woman on the frontier—or does it matter at all? To be sure there is much we do not know about the Bryans and many unsolved questions which arouses an ongoing interest in this family. Luckily, to the credit and appreciation of the diligent research of others and by strong family tradition, we know that Rebecca had a solid connection to the British Isles, which gives me a good starting place.

VIRGINIA

Rebecca was born in 1739 under the rein of King George II near present day Winchester, Virginia, in the lower part of the Shenandoah Valley. At the time of her birth this place was a part of Orange County but by 1743 the newly formed county of Frederick became her home. Although the Church of England was the official church of Virginia, colonial officials were tolerant to other religious groups settling in the back parts. By the year 1738, Presbyterians, Quakers, Lutherans, and Anglicans were becoming established in the settlement called Fredrick Town. It is here that we can find some of the oldest churches in the Shenandoah Valley including Hopewell Meeting House, established in 1734.

In 1730 Rebecca's grandfather, Morgan Bryan partnered with Ross Alexander in a land deal acquiring 100,000 acres from Governor Gooch to establish a Quaker settlement. Bryan was the businessman and Alexander was the agent to attract Friends to the new land. This tract was situated on Opequon Creek, a tributary of the Potomac River and in close proximity to a path called the Indian Road. Available farmland in Pennsylvania and Maryland was becoming scarce, creating a high market value thus causing settlers and land speculators to look westward for cheap fertile land.

In 1734 Bryan purchased another nearby tract where he and his large family lived, including Rebecca's parents, Joseph and Hester Bryan. This is believed to be the birthplace of Rebecca Ann Bryan.

The route into this unknown wilderness was nothing more than a glorified footpath, trodden by centuries of hoof prints from roaming animal herds. It became a well-known Native American pathway for trading, hunting, and warring with rival tribes all the way from the Carolinas to the Great Lakes. From Philadelphia the path went westward to Lancaster, York, and Hagerstown

Maryland. At Watkins Ferry the trail crossed the Potomac dropping south to what we know today as Winchester, Virginia.

The loveliness of the valley stretched far away in every direction: hills and dells, gently rolling ridges, groves of chestnut, bold streams, open lands with tall grasses, Allegheny ranges to the west, and towering Massanuttens to the south. This unspoiled paradise was once hunting grounds to the Shawnee and other tribes. Big game still roamed the valley—elk, bear, panther, deer, wolves, beaver, otter, soaring eagles, and perhaps even buffalo. Panthers, wolves, and wild cats were so troublesome to the settlements that the colonial authorities paid bounties for the hides. Portions of the valley floor was rich, fertile limestone perfect for grain, corn, and hay cultivation. There was slate earth too, well suited for growing wheat and fruits. This was the landscape of young Rebecca Bryan in her early years before moving to Carolina.

Records of Rebecca's mother are unclear and sometimes confusing. It is believed that Rebecca's mother was Hester Hampton and that she died about 1740, during or shortly after the birth of her second daughter, Martha. Upon her death, the care of Rebecca and Martha was probably taken on by her grandmother Martha Bryan along with the older girls in the Bryan household. Within a year her father Joseph married Alice Linville and it is presumed that he stayed behind with his new family before joining his father later in North Carolina. Rebecca was about 7 or 8 years old when Morgan Bryan's clan decided to pull up stakes and move south to Big Lick which is now Roanoke. The 175 mile journey was difficult.

Written accounts reveal very slow movement. In some places trees had to be cut to allow wagons the space to move. We do not know in what fashion the family traveled, whether by pack horses, two wheeled carts or in big conestoga wagons, perhaps all of these. By any imagination the journey was arduous, making perhaps as little as 5 miles a day, maybe more if the path was easier. Whatever supplies were needed had to be carried with them for there was no hope of obtaining them once leaving the last settlement. At Big Lick the Bryans stopped and stayed put for several months. William Bryan decided to settle there while Morgan and his family loaded up and continued pushing south on the Carolina Road to the Yadkin Valley.

Traveling from the Roanoke River to the Yadkin was probably the most difficult section of the Bryans' journey. Morgan, in his mid-seventies, and his sons, hacked their way through a wilderness. It took the family three months to reach Shallow Ford on the Yadkin. The road was terrible through Maggoty Gap to the east side of the Blue Ridge. Morgan wrote that the wagon had to be disassemble and carried piecemeal up the last incline. When the Moravians came to Bethabara in 1753, they used

Upper Yadkin River

the road the Bryans blazed. Rebecca experienced in her very young life the hardships of living in a wilderness. Those lessons she secured prepared her for the life she would eventually share with Daniel Boone.

ON THE YADKIN

The Bryans were one of the first families that settled in Forks of the Yadkin on the North Carolina frontier. This fork is the land that lies between the South Fork of the Yadkin and the Yadkin. They arrived in 1749 when Rebecca was about 10 years old. A noted explorer, John Lawson wrote in his journal from the early 1700's that "this land was a pleasant savanna having very few trees with fine bladed grass six feet high along the rivers and streams."

There was an abundance of wild game and fish. The air was fresh and sweet; the Yadkin clear and rocky. This was to be Rebecca's home for the next twenty years or more.

Apparently Bryan's previous land dealings had made him a prosperous man thus making it possible to bring all the supplies necessary to make a new beginning in an uninhabited place. Carefully stored in wagons or packed on horses might be spinning wheels, looms, linen and wool, straight pens and needles, crocks, iron cook pots, salt, paper, hemp, barrels, wagon and horse tack, blacksmith, carpentry, and farm tools, axes, adzes, flour, cornmeal, hams, clothing, grains, cooking utensils, garden seeds, apple and cherry saplings, muskets, blackpowder, and lead. Oxen, horses, chickens, geese, and sheep probably joined the caravan as well.

Within a few years the Bryans acquired substantial land holdings along Deep Creek, above the Shallow Ford on the Yadkin River. When the German speaking Moravians settled their Wachovia tract in 1752 at Bethabara the area west of the Yadkin was already known as the "Bryan Settlements."

Rebecca was part of a very large family; sister Martha, father Joseph and stepmother Alice, half siblings, cousins, aunts, uncles, and her beloved grandparents. Her grandmother Martha Strode must have been a strong and caring woman

A view of the Yadkin River

who had children of her own plus Rebecca, and who knows how many others to guide and instruct. Rebecca would have been taught from an early age to do simple chores and as she grew older was able to help with household and farm chores such as washing dishes, making butter, carding wool, spinning, weaving, fetching firewood, gathering nuts and berries, picking vegetables from the garden, sewing and taking care of the younger children. She would learn by watching and by example. The men of the family were felling trees for log cabins and barns, clearing fields, plowing, making furniture, hunting, and tanning hides. Rebecca increased her knowledge and skills by observing her elders.

THE BOONES TO CAROLINA

By 1752 Squire Boone and his family had also found their way from Berks County, Pennsylvania, to the Yadkin Valley. Daniel was a young lad in his late teens. The Boones, like thousands of others, were moving into the Carolina Piedmont searching for cheap fertile land. In 1753 Squire paid only 3 shillings for 640 acres on Bear Creek near present day Mocksville.

Daniel learned blacksmithing and weaving skills from his father. He also helped with farming, surveying, and road building but his most rewarding occupation soon became hunting. Deer were plentiful and their hides were becoming a valuable export commodity. Hard currency was extremely scarce in the backcountry. No coins were being minted in the colonies. The Spanish milled dollar, pieces of eight, and English coins were the most common. What soon became a replacement for currency was a buck deer hide valued at a dollar. Pack horses laden with hides were brought into Salisbury for export and trade.

In the many years to follow, a shared faith and geography led to many marriages between the two families, creating a strong Bryan-Boone clan.

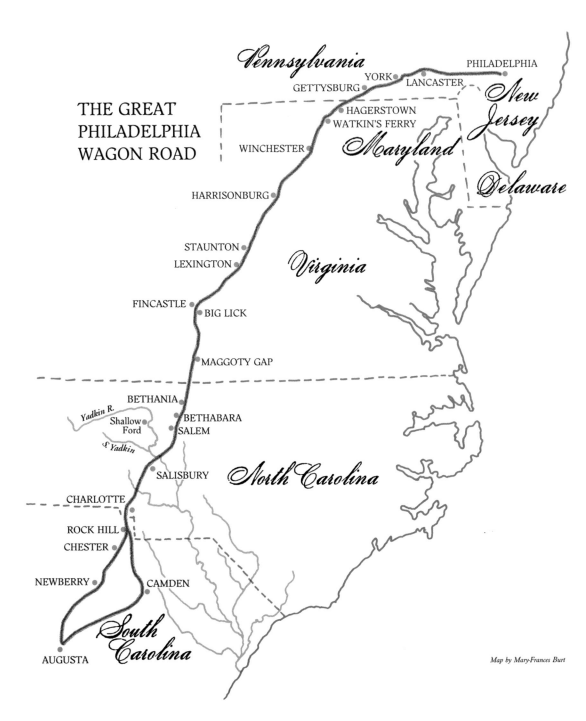

THE GREAT
PHILADELPHIA
WAGON ROAD

Pennsylvania

PHILADELPHIA

YORK · LANCASTER

GETTYSBURG

New Jersey

HAGERSTOWN

WATKIN'S FERRY

WINCHESTER

Maryland

Delaware

HARRISONBURG

STAUNTON

LEXINGTON

Virginia

FINCASTLE

BIG LICK

MAGGOTY GAP

BETHANIA

Yadkin R.

Shallow
Ford

BETHABARA

SALEM

S. Yadkin

SALISBURY

North Carolina

CHARLOTTE

ROCK HILL

CHESTER

NEWBERRY

CAMDEN

South Carolina

AUGUSTA

Map by Mary-Frances Burt

THE GREAT PHILADELPHIA WAGON ROAD

The Great Wagon Road, stretching from Philadelphia to Augusta, Georgia, was the most important transportation link in colonial America. Vast numbers of German, English and Scots Irish traveled the road to reach new land in the Carolinas. Seven hundred thirty miles in length, it boasted rocks, pot holes, stumps, mud, dust, swollen creeks, and wide rivers. Some people referred to it as the Bad Road. From Roanoke at Big Lick it was called the Carolina Road.

Travel inland to the back parts of the colonies was near impossible from the coastal ports. The wagon road through the Valley of Virginia opened up the lands to the west. Land in Pennsylvania was becoming more and more scarce, and if available, prohibitively expensive. Land in the Carolinas was good and cheap, albeit getting there was slow and rugged. On a good day, wagon drawn by teams of oxen or horses could make about 15 miles a day. The trip from Pennsylvania to the Yadkin usually took about six weeks.

During the early settlement of America, colonists used paths and trails already established by Native Americans. The ancient Great Warriors Path was used

1753 GREAT PHILADELPHIA WAGON ROAD

The most heavily traveled in Colonial America passed near here, linking areas from The Great Lakes to Augusta, GA. Laid out on animal and Native American Trading & Warrior Paths. Indian treaties among NY, PA, VA and the Iroquois League of Five Nations in 1685 and 1722 opened Colonial Backcountry for peaceful settlement along this road of the Piedmont.

NATIONAL SOCIETY DAUGHTERS OF THE AMERICAN COLONISTS. PROJECT OF THE 2000-3 ADMINISTRATION.

by the Iroquois, Cherokees, and Catawba for trading or to make war on rival tribes. Native Americans followed paths originally worn by roaming herds of animals such as deer and woods buffalo. The woods buffalo were shaggy and roamed in groups of two or three, usually a cow and calves. They grazed on cane-breaks and followed ridges and along creek banks. In 1744 the Virginia assembly, by a series of treaties with the Five Nations of the Iroquois, acquired the use of the trail.

In the early years pioneers with meager belongings used pack horses, walked, or rode horseback following the narrow foot path. Some places were no more than 3-4 feet wide. When more and more settlers came, the road was widened in some places to 35 feet, enough for 2 wagons to pass.

One frosty November morning in 2004, I met up with some some Yadkin County history buffs in Huntsville not far from the east side of Shallow Ford on the Yadkin. Our goal was to make our way down to the river's edge using the wagon path that was known as Mulberry Fields Road. With boots, walking sticks, and cameras, we were led through woods, fields and thickets to the wagon crossing. Shallow Ford is located on the Yadkin/Forsyth County line. The ravages of time and the ever-changing river made the site of the path obscure. We were searching for the steep ravine that had been cut by years of continuous use of wagons and horses coming out of the river. The ford is called Shallow because it is a low rocky place in the river. It has been used for hundreds of years by Native Americans and wild-life. The crossing is at an angle from east to southwest, south of the Shallowford Road bridge.

Rebecca's Larder

A well stocked larder would have been of upmost importance to a mother caring for young children in the back settlements whose man was often away on hunting forays. The larder was a place to keep food items safe and away from vermin. Often it was part of the house—a room designed for storing food, a cellar, shelves suspended from the rafters, or just flat boards placed on pegs along the cabin walls. For provisions that kept best at lower temperatures a larder in the coolest part of the house and low to the ground was necessary. Floors may have been large slab stones, brick or just dirt. Cheese, pickled foods, butter, eggs, and root crops may have been part of Rebecca's food stores. Crocks, stone jars, spice boxes, horn cups, gourds, or leather pouches would fill the shelves. Crocks would have been covered with wood planks, hog bladders or leather tied with heavy string or hemp. We may not know for certain what was on Rebecca's pantry shelves but based on writings of the times we can make some good assumptions. Salt, cornmeal, flour, lard or bear oil would have been common and essential stores.

Other items could have included oats, spices, tea, maple syrup, maple sugar, molasses, honey, sugar, salted meats, pickled vegetables, dried fruits and meats. Black tea, sugar, molasses and spices were expensive imported staples and would have been traded for, or purchased in Salisbury, Bethabara, or Salem. If Rebecca had any of these luxury items it is possible that Daniel traded hides for them. Imported goods came into the interior of the colony by way of Cross Creek on the Cape Fear River, Charles Towne on the coast, or the Wagon Road from Philadelphia. Keep in mind, most foods available in the backcountry would have been grown or produced on the farm or within the community.

MOLASSES

Molasses is a by-product of the sugar making process. In the 18th century it was produced in the West Indies—sometimes called the British Sugar Islands—from sugar cane and imported into the colonies. This product was not the sorghum molasses we have here in the South today. Sorghum is a cereal grain that came into wide spread production in America for making syrup starting in the mid-nineteenth century. Prior to that molasses was imported under British regulations to the colonies from sugar plantations.

The kind of molasses in Rebecca's day would have been light or dark molasses produced from sugar cane juice. Molasses was not only used as a sweetener but in the manufacturing of dark rum.

Juice from the crushed sugar cane was boiled down and evaporated leaving sugar crystals in the dark syrup. The syrup was then placed in large wooden kegs that had holes in the bottom allowing a filtering process much like a colander. The residue left in the kegs was raw sugar crystals. It was the first of many processes in the production of refined sugar. Syrup from the first boiling of cane juice is light molasses. The second boiling produces a darker syrup and the third boiling produces a dark bitter syrup called Black Strap Molasses, usually not used for cooking.

Molasses blends well with hearty grains like cornmeal and whole wheat flour. It was a key ingredient in making ginger breads and cakes. Molasses goes well on hot buttered corn cakes, Indian mush, or porridge.

SUGAR

In colonial America many early settlers were using dark molasses, honey or maple syrup for sweeteners. The lengthy procedures in producing sugar made it prohibitively expensive. The more refined, the higher the cost. This was a food for the wealthy. Not only was sugar expensive it was not readily available on the frontier.

Raw sugar or natural sugar was imported to New England where it could be sold in lumps cheaper than refined. There were a number of establishments that further refined the crystals molding it into a conical shape that became very hard. The cones of different weights were wrapped in blue paper and tied with string. The blue paper made the sugar appear much whiter and increased its appeal. Sugar packaged this way was called loaf sugar.

Homespun foods from the hearths of the back settlers did not require sugar. This was a luxury item and I have often wondered how much sugar was on Rebecca's shelf or if there was any at all.

SALT

Of course we do not know all the items stored in Rebecca's kitchen, but the one absolute essential was salt. Today it may be hard to imagine the importance of salt in the everyday life of colonial ancestors. It is a necessary nutrient for the health of humans as well as for livestock. Salt was equally important as a preservative of meat.

North Carolina colonial records show that in 1775 the Provisional Congress passed three laws related to salt aiming to regulate prices, help ensure against shortages and establishing salt manufacturing in North Carolina.

At the beginning of the Revolution, the Continental Congress noted that salt was as necessary to the survival of the country as were arms and ammunition and that if it could not be imported it would need to be manufactured here. During the war, salt was sometimes part of the payment to soldiers. (The Latin root word for salary is salt.)

During colonial times, salt shipped into Wilmington was brought up the Cape Fear River to Cross Creek which today is Fayetteville.

Cross Creek was a trading center for the import and export of commodities for settlers in the interior of the colony. Backcountry farmers and merchants could acquire salt and other items by the exchange of flour, hides, or the like. There are other references of salt being brought into southwestern Virginia by wagons from Williamsburg. Cross Creek was about 130 miles from Salisbury and Salem and another 60 or more miles to the upper Yadkin settlements near Mulberry Fields, present day Wilkesboro. Frontiersmen could also make their own salt supply from salt licks and salt springs.

Salt was made by boiling water from salt springs or ocean water until only the salt crystals remained. This was done in large iron kettles. The ratio of gallons of water to a gallon of salt varied and depended on the saline strength in the water. A strong saline solution of 80 gallons could produce a gallon of salt. This was an unrefined salt not like the pure white salts we find on our shelves today.

MAPLE SYRUP & MAPLE SUGAR

Most people associate maple syrup with Vermont and other New England states, but during the 18th century and even today maple syrup can be made in North Carolina. Moravian records state that in January 1754 settlers boiled sap from nearby maple trees to make syrup. Ten years later in another account, they noted the syrup was so sweet that some sugar could be boiled from it and so plentiful that some used it as a drink. From this we know that maple syrup was being made in the area and there is no reason to doubt that the Boones and Bryans were making it as well.

Rebecca and Daniel lived for a time on Sugar Tree Creek near the present community of Farmington in Davie County.

It is believed that the name Sugar Tree is attributed to the abundance of maples along the waters. The latter part of the 1700's experienced unusually cold winters which would create excellent conditions for making syrup. For me, it is easy to imagine that Rebecca had kegs or stone jars of maple syrup and even maple sugar in her larder.

I have been fortunate to use locally made maple syrup and maple sugar as ingredients for baking at Rebecca's replicated hearth at Whippoorwill Village in Ferguson. Homemade maple syrup is a delight to have on hot buttered corn cakes. The sugar can be used in making pies and little cakes or cookies. Making syrup was not such an easy task for the backcountry settlers but it was cheaper and easier to obtain than imported sugar.

SPICES

What spices Rebecca Boone may have had in her pantry is only a guess. Spices were precious and costly commodities in eighteenth century America and would have been hard to obtain in the back settlements.

Cinnamon, cloves, nutmeg, vanilla beans, and ginger were shipped to coastal towns from the Spice Islands. Allspice—also called Pimento or Jamaica Pepper—and Cayenne Pepper came from the West Indies. All came unrefined, packed in casks. It is a good to know that whole spices retain their flavor better over a period of time for it could be months from the time the spices were harvested until they reached the cabin shelf. Graters, mortar and pestles, and spice mills were used to grind or pound the spices into fine powder.

Because of their value, like sugar, they were often put in locked boxes for safekeeping. Surprisingly, pepper is said to have been the spice most sought after.

CORNMEAL AND FLOUR

Water grist mills were a necessary establishment in every community and were usually situated on fast running creeks or natural falls. As early as 1758 the North Carolina legislature took measures to encourage the construction of mills, directed the duties of millers, and took greater supervision over the operation of public mills. Anyone desiring to build a mill would first petition the local court and obtain leave for such a mill. Millers were to grind according to turn and to grind well and sufficient the grain brought to their mill. One half bushel and one peck measurements were tried and stamped by the Keeper of the Standard of the county—2 toll dishes for each measure—one for wheat and one for corn. 1/8th part of the wheat and 1/6th part of the Indian corn went to the miller. Should a miller be found abusing the system, a fine of 15 shillings proclamation money could be imposed. The importance of this industry is reflected by the actions taken by the colonial assembly.

Corn was one of the most important crops grown in early North Carolina, and some will say the most important. It was versatile, used to feed both farm animals and pioneer families. By-products were useful around the farm as well: corn shucks for mattresses, mops, or dolls. Fodder was feed for livestock and corncobs were good for scrubbing pots. There are some varieties of heritage corn available today. Indian corn, Dent corn, and Bloody Butcher corn are examples and may be as close as we can get to the kind of corn our 18th ancestors used. Stone ground meal was made into cornbread, mush, Indian pudding, corn pones, Indian slapjacks and ash cakes. Corn could be parched, boiled, roasted, ground, or made into hominy and was easier to grow than wheat.

Wheat produced the hearty English breads Rebecca's family would have enjoyed. One example of heritage seed is Red May which is an old variety much like Yellow Lammas, a European winter wheat. The production of wheat was a long process from the field to the table which may have been the reason it had a higher market value than corn. We may not know if the Boones grew wheat but from the Moravian records we do know that it was being grown and could be purchased.

It is easy to imagine that Rebecca had a good supply of bear oil in her larder. A Tennessee back woodsmen once told me that anything you can do with a hog you can do with a bear: make bacon and ham, tan the hide for leather, and render the fat to oil. The oil can be used for cooking, cleaning a rifle, or rubbing on leather goods to preserve them. The Moravians mention that they used bear oil for cooking and that it had a sweet taste. I have used bear oil to season my skillet before cooking corn cakes and the like and it works fine. I feel certain Rebecca had containers of this oil on her shelf.

KITCHEN GARDEN

Most farmsteads had a fenced herb and vegetable garden close to the cabin door and Rebecca's would have been be no different. When she and Daniel moved from the Bryan settlements to her upper Yadkin River homesites she would have brought seeds and diggings of herbs with her. These gardens were situated close to the cabin for convenience and fenced to keep out free roaming pigs, cows, chickens, and wildlife. The types of fences varied— picket, wattle, or brush.

A wattle fence is made out of sapling trees, branches, cane, or vines—anything that could be woven like a basket. They could be constructed with the use of a hatch or sturdy knife and could be very uniform and tailored or rustic. Using whatever materials were at hand was the simplest and fastest way to establish a barrier for a garden. The Boone children could have easily accomplished this task.

The size of the gardens varied and often was decided by the size of the family. Here is a sampling of frontier garden vegetables, herbs, and field crops based on records of the nearby Moravians.

Vegetables: Onions, Chives, Parsley, Cucumbers, Dill, Leeks,

Lettuce, Cauliflower, Beets, Parsnips, Endive, Spinach, Cress, Carrot, Beans, Rhubarb, Cabbage, Rutabaga

Herbs: Lemon Balm, Marjoram, Thyme, Basil, Catnip, Comfrey, Lavender, Chamomile, Rue, Sage, Tansy, Wormwood, Yarrow, Rosemary

Field crops: Corn, Wheat, Turnips, Pumpkins, Barley, Hops, Oats, Potatoes

Fruits: Apples, Cherries, Gooseberries, Pears, Peaches, Grapes

LIVING OFF THE LAND

As I think about Rebecca living in a wilderness setting I ponder on the kinds of wild foods she could have relied upon to add to, or supplement, the meals for her large family.

Wild game was plentiful —squirrel, rabbit, deer, bear, possibly elk, fish, turkey, duck, crawfish, and pigeons. Wild game could have been used in place of a ham bone for seasoning, roasted or in stews.

Berries and nuts included red mulberry, pawpaws, wild strawberries, plums, blackberries, persimmons, crabapple, grapes, hickory nuts, black walnuts, and chestnuts.

Wild greens grew in the rich bottomlands of the Yadkin Valley. Greens that could be added to the pot include polk, yellow dock, dandelion, winter cress, chickweed, wild mustard, and sorrel. The Boone cooks may have also used turnip roots and greens, collards, mustard, or kale in recipes.

If you are using wild greens, be certain that what you have picked is edible. Wild greens can sometimes have a bitter taste. You may want to parboil them and then drain before adding them to the meat stock.

Open Hearth Cooking

Open-hearth cooking is the practice of cooking food in the fireplace by the heat of the flames or on the hearth by using hot coals. Cook pots for boiling and stewing are hung on the arm of a crane or on a rod over the fire, while baking is done in Dutch-ovens on the hearth. Hot coals placed under the three-legged pot and piled on the lid provide conditions for baking much like a modern oven.

Large fireplaces in homes of long ago were an essential that provided warmth, light, and a means to cook food. The hearth was the central focus of the home and the place at which the family gathered. Modern fireplaces are not usually built of necessity but rather they are for the pleasure of a cozy fire or purely for aesthetics. However, when the lights and heat go out,

having a functional fireplace and being able to utilize it to its fullest can be a life saver.

The cold days of winter present a perfect time to try your hand at cooking on the hearth. Although cooking in this manner takes considerable more time and patience than using the conveniences of modern kitchens, it has its own rewards. There is an art to cooking on the open hearth and you can master it. Following these few basic tips will get you off to a great start!

BASIC SAFETY TIPS

Have a fire extinguisher nearby and know how to use it (colonial cooks used a water bucket). Wear appropriate clothes—avoid synthetic clothing and items such as long flowing skirts, loose shirts, dangling jewelry. Try cottons and linens, jeans and a sweatshirt. Wear shoes that will protect the feet. Tie back long hair. Have pot hooks or other means to lift hot lids from Dutch-ovens. Do not use your hands even if you have on an oven mitt. The coals produce high heat and are very hot, even if the embers are not bright red. Don't get in a hurry. Colonial cooks did not have clocks and timers.

GETTING STARTED

First start with the fire and remember big is not better. Aim for hot coals, not a big flame. Allow fire to burn about one hour before starting to cook. Use seasoned hard woods like hickory, oak, or maple, which produce the hottest coals. Use cast iron cookware. Heavy cast iron holds and evenly distributes heat. Dutch-ovens come in various sizes but a good basic size is a 12-inch diameter that is four or five inches deep. Pots should be seasoned before cooking. If you are using a new pot sometimes they come preseasoned. Preheat pots by placing them near the fire, inside the fireplace. Lids can be propped up against the inside walls of the fireplace. This process is the same as preheating a modern day oven. A long handle shovel will be needed to scoop coals onto the hearth and onto the lid of the Dutch-oven.

IT'S IN THE POT

When the bread or other dish is ready for baking, shovel a small pile of red hot coals onto the hearth, but not close to the outside edge of the hearth. Next place a flat trivet or put three small pebbles in the bottom of the Dutch-oven for the pan to sit on. This allows air to circulate under the pan and more evenly distributes the heat. Place the Dutch-oven on top of the coals. Next, place the pan of bread dough in the pot. An oven-safe baking dish or a round cake pan works well. Put the lid on the pot securely and shovel hot coals onto the lid. "Cook until done," is a quote found in many old cookbooks. Because the temperature of the oven is unknown, judging the length of time to bake can be tricky. Check the bread periodically and notice the smell. Another old saying from generations long ago is that the cook can tell if something is done by the way it smells. Based on experience it may take 30 minutes or more, depending on the heat of the coals, to completely bake a loaf of bread. If the bread is not browning as it should add more hot coals underneath or on top of the Dutch-oven.

CAST IRON POTS

Where to get 'em and how to take care of 'em

Some folks say that food cooked in iron pots at the fireplace or on the wood stove tastes better. It really does! Nothing cooks better than a well-seasoned and well used cast iron skillet or Dutch-oven. Whether it is for frying or baking you can't beat them and you sure can't wear them out. The trick is to have a cast iron pot that is made well and to keep it seasoned. The seasoning process protects the pots from rusting and gives them a non-stick surface.

Looking for good cast iron cookware? Start by asking older family members. Back in the days when everyone had a wood stove or cooked on the hearth the cookware of the day was cast iron. Some may be hidden away that can be cleaned up and put back into service. Maybe you like finding treasures at flea markets and antique sales. Look for quality, one that is made all in one piece, bottoms and sides joined smoothly and without a welded seam. The inner surface of skillets should be smooth with no signs of deep scratches or gouges. If you should find one with a slight sheen, then you'll know you have found one that has been used and cared for properly.

New pots can be purchased at some general hardware stores, camping supply stores, or online. The best known maker of cast iron cookware is Lodge Cast Iron. It is the oldest family owned cookware foundry in the U.S. They offer a large selection of cook pots. Avoid thin cast iron products. Heavier is better even though you'll need a strong arm and wrist. In addition, you will have something to pass down as an heirloom. Proper care for cast iron cookware is essential for successful cooking. Even those new pots that come pre-seasoned could benefit from the seasoning process. First, wash pots in hot sudsy water. Scrub with steel wool if necessary to get a smooth clean surface. Avoid putting detergent directly on cast iron and never put cast iron into the dishwasher. After washing, rinse well, pat dry with cloth or paper towel. Some cooks prefer to place pots in a warm oven for a minute to thoroughly dry them. Next, give your pots a generous protective coating of unsalted grease or oil inside and out, but give more care to the inner surface. Traditionally lard and suet were used. Place cookware in a 200-250° oven, for two hours. If cookware begins to smoke the oven is too hot. Keep a watch on the cookware as it seasons to see if oil runs or puddles. Use a paper towel to wipe oil or grease evenly and apply more grease if a pot absorbs all of it within two hours. Pots are seasoned if they look shiny black. Turn off oven and let pots remain until oven has cooled. Wipe pots again to remove any excess oil. After cooking in the Dutch-oven or skillet, rinse pots with hot water or wipe with clean cloth. Sometimes I use a wooden or plastic scraper, but no soap. Make sure pots are thoroughly dry before storing. Keep cookware away from dampness, as it may cause it to become rusty. Cast iron cookware may need to be reseasoned from time to time— simply repeat the process.

MORDECAI HOUSE

ALLEN KITCHEN
RALEIGH, NC

The Allen Kitchen is on the grounds of Mordecai Historic Park in Raleigh, one half mile north of the Capitol off Wake Forest Road. It is situated in a peaceful oasis amid the busy streets of downtown. The circa 1842 kitchen was moved to its present location from Anson County, North Carolina, as a complement to the historic Mordecai House.

It was when I was the State Tar Heel Junior Historian Program Coordinator at the North Carolina Museum of History that I discovered this soft yellow framed kitchen. My volunteer times there included useful endeavors of visiting the wood pile, starting the cook fire, sweeping the floor, and preparing the kitchen table for the day. It was a privilege to provide simple cooking classes for children and heritage cooking demonstrations for visitors. The classes for youngsters was especially rewarding as we all worked together mixing cornmeal, fetching water, shelling peas, rolling out pie dough, setting the table and even washing and drying dishes.

Children's cooking class

Winter days offered snow filtered air with brilliant blue skies and the scent of smoke swirling up the chimney. On Spring mornings the sun shone warmly through the wavy window panes. Pink and white blossoms, Easter shades of grass and a white picket fenced herb garden provided a beautiful setting equal to Colonial Williamsburg. Strolling through the kitchen garden was a refreshing exercise of examining, naming, smelling and tenderly brushing my fingers against the leaves or flowers.

Picking tanzy in the kitchen garden

ALLEN KITCHEN GARDEN

BOONE CABIN
WHIPPOORWILL ACADEMY • FERGUSON, NC

orking at the hearth of the replica Boone cabin gives me a feeling of being connected— immersed with imaginations and thoughts of Rebecca Boone whose home was nearby. It was here, through the inspiration of Edith Marie Carter, that the seed of preparing these writings was planted. In 2006 Mrs. Carter asked me to do a cooking demonstration for her annual Daniel Boone Day. It was an opportunity to weave together fireplace cooking and the story of Rebecca. That first year black eyed peas seasoned with pork, greens and cornbread was the

fare of the day. Each year more
dishes were added; cherry tarts,
cinnamon pie, onion pie, seed
cake, Abigail's ginger cakes, and
sugar plums. The sight and smell of
fireplace smoke seems to encourage
visitors to drift toward Rebecca's
cabin. Conversations lingered
around the hearth with stories and
memories of someone's granny
cooking in cast iron pots.

One of my best cooking days at
Whippoorwill was a cold December
Christmas event. The day's high
was 32 with a bit of a stiff wind but
the fireplace was warm and flick-
ered a golden light across the cabin.
Magnolia leaves and cedar boughs

M   47

BOONE TRACT

In 1753 Lord Granville
granted 640 acres on Bear
Creek to Squire Boone
who sold it in 1759 to his
son Daniel. This was a part
of the original Boone tract.

DIVISION OF ARCHIVES AND HISTORY   1979

At right: Preparing a stuffed pumpkin.

graced the mantel around the glow of candles. A white linen cloth covered the work table on which ginger cakes were served from pewter plates set off with a sprig of holly. Aromas of spices from the cookies baking in the Dutch-oven filled the room with a sweet spirit. How I wish Rebecca could have been with me. The reproduced Boone cabin is representative of the kind of home the Boones' had on the banks of the Yadkin. Its size

. . . .

*Above: A goat at Wippoorwill.
Below: Pottery jugs, cast iron pot and butter churn at Boone Cabin.*

was based upon Mrs. Carter's grandfather's measurements of the field stone corners at the original site taken over 70 years ago. Some of the original stones are on display here. It is very possible that this Boone cabin site was the last home Daniel and Rebecca lived in before moving to Kentucky. The cabin is one of several log structures located at the Whippoorwill Village on North Carolina Highway 268 about twelve miles west of Wilkesboro on the upper Yadkin.

From top to bottom: The Boone Cabin mantel decorated for Christmas. A Seed cake (Recipe, page 134). Abigail's Ginger Cakes (Recipe, page 141).

GINGERBREAD MEN

CLEVELAND HOUSE

WILKES HERITAGE MUSEUM • WILKESBORO, NC

Cooking at the Cleveland Hearth has been one of the joys of my cooking journey. The two story log dwelling built in 1779 was the home of Aley and Robert Cleveland and their thirteen children. Robert was a Captain in the Wilkes Militia and fought at the Battle of Kings Mountain along with his brother Colonel Benjamin Cleveland. In 1986 the structure was moved from the Parsonville community to the Wilkes Heritage Museum and restored. It is oldest house in Wilkes County. The stone fireplace and hearth in this historic house provides an excellent place to cook. It has been an honor to have been asked many times to demonstrate heritage cooking there. Knowing that I am working in a patriot family's home is very meaningful. In addition to that, I live only a short distance from the original homesite of the Clevelands' and so, if I had been living back then, Aley and I may have been neighbors. It is also very possible that the Clevelands and Boones were acquainted as the Boone Cabin on the Yadkin is in close proximity. It is said that Ben Cleveland learned much about Kentucky from Daniel Boone.

There are not enough fingers and toes to count the times I have started an early morning cook fire in Aley's hearth. In the old days it was not usually necessary to start a new fire each morning as the coals from the previous day would have been banked at night so only a few dry twigs or kindling would have been needed to catch up the coals the next morning. The solid walnut cook table was specially built for the Cleveland House by Frank Parlier, a master craftsman. It is one of the most beautiful pieces of reproduction furniture I have seen.

In preparation and planning for cooking classes and demonstrations at the museum I always think of Aley Cleveland. She, like Rebecca Boone, was a frontier woman with a lot of mouths to feed. Both women lived in the Yadkin Valley. What foods might have been prepared at the hearth for so large a family? What crops were grown here? What supplies were in Aley's larder?

Receipts for cooking classes have included Black Caps, Ordinary Bread, Chickweed Sallet, Turnips and Greens, Chicken with Dumplins and Cole Slaw.

For holidays, Gingerbread Boys baked in the Dutch-oven filled the cabin with a wistful aroma of Christmases long ago. Stuffed pumpkin prepared in the 18th century manner was a treat as well. Other favorites included Roast Goose, Scottish Shortbread, and Another Sort of Cake.

Opposite: Stuffed pumpkin and gingerbread. Above: baked apples. Right: a cheerful fire prepared for visitors.

HAGGOTT HOUSE

HAGGOTT HOUSE
HIGH POINT MUSEUM • HIGH POINT, NC

My experience at the hearth of the Haggott House was a bit unusual. Not every cooking day is a perfect success. This particular day was the 1993 Christmas living history event for the High Point Museum. I was to cook a goose and plum sauce. Somehow in packing up I left a basket of kitchen utensils and dishes at home. As I had traveled a good distance to High Point, going back to get them was not an option. At times we just have to "make do."

The Haggott House is a simple log dwelling built about 1801 by the youngest son of Philip and Mary Haggott who migrated to Piedmont North Carolina with other Quaker families in the late 1700s. It was a lovely setting with a glowing fire and two open doorways convenient for the flow of visitors. I never knew why, but a large group of international families came for that Christmas event. Their fascination with cooking in the fireplace resulted in some lengthy,

Above: Mary demonstrates Christmas cooking at Haggott House

pleasant conversations between us. Roasted goose was a good choice for interpreting food-ways of a family with English roots. Along with the goose I prepared a tasty plumb sauce. Since the platter and some of the serving dishes were not with me, the goose had to be presented in the Dutch-oven and the sauce in the redware pipkin in which each was cooked. The table was not set as I had planned which caused me some consternation, yet the story of the forgotten serving dishes and tableware seemed to add some humor to the day and visitors did not seem to be concerned at all.

On another occasion I taught simple cooking for a children's colonial camp. It was summer and hot but the youngsters seemed to enjoy it immensely. Over the three days we cooked corn cakes, ham, corn on the cob, and little cakes. The last day we cut into a juicy watermelon and ate it the old-fashioned way.

Colonial cooking is a great way to get children's attention, and along with the fun, weave in some valuable history lessons.

LATTA HOUSE

LATTA PLANTATION
CATAWBA RIVER PLANTATION • HUNTERSVILLE, NC

A backcountry log cabin at Latta Place is where my cooking journey began. Latta Place is a Catawba River Plantation, located on Mountain Island Lake northwest of Charlotte, dating back to 1800. The Federal style home of James Latta and his wife Jane Knox features extraordinary interior architecture and looks more like a Philadelphia townhouse than a Southern plantation dwelling. Today Latta Plantation is a well-developed working plantation offering various interpretive programs and events for visitors throughout the year.

I first became acquainted with Latta in 1983 when I enrolled in a log cabin construction class through Central Piedmont Community College.

Under the instruction of Don Chapman, our class built a yeomen farmer's cabin that was representative of the kind of dwelling ordinary farmers in the area might have had. The cabin was built as much as possible in the old way, by hand. We gathered field stones for the corner pillars, some of which were so heavy they required two or three students to carry. The men cut poplar and oaks from the neighboring

woods and all of us pitched
in to manually carry those
sap-laden logs up to the site
using timber tongs. Chain saws
were used to fell the trees but
after that it was back to the
broad axe and adze. During

*Above: This was the first time I
cooked in the cabin I helped build
at Latta Plantation. Right: On one
occasion at Latta the weather
was so bitterly cold our dish pan
water turned to ice during our
evening meal. In order to wash
the dishes, a kettle of water had
to be heated up on the fire just to
warm the dish water.*

those building sessions it was as if we had escaped into a long ago world. It was the hardest work I have ever done. Three years later I began cooking in the cabin I helped build and I loved it.

A buttermilk cornbread receipt from a treasured period cookbook was my first attempt at cooking on the hearth. The golden brown cornbread was beautiful and delicious.

During my times at Latta I cooked many different kinds of dishes over the cabin hearth including pies, puddings, roast shad, pork pie, and Jane Latta's gingerbread.

Above: British regiment reenactors make a toast during a winter event commemorating the crossing of Lord Cornwallis over the Catawba River and the Battle of Cowan's Ford, February 1, 1781. The ford was very close to the dam on Lake Norman, not far from Latta Plantation.

William Lee Davidson was killed at the battle. He is the patriot for whom Davidson College is named.

MABRY MILL
Courtesy Library of Congress

MATTHEWS CABIN

MABRY MILL • BLUE RIDGE PARKWAY, VA

he Blue Ridge Parkway holds a special place in my heart. I love riding the crest of the mountains and feel a reverence passing through gaps along fenced pastures and open vistas. Being asked to cook at the Matthews' fireplace at Mabry Mill was a rare opportunity and one that gave me great pleasure.

The one-and-a-half story traditional Appalachian cabin was built in 1869 and was the home of Samuel and Elizabeth Matthews. In 1956 family descendants donated it to the Blue Ridge Parkway. It was moved from the Mount Lebanon Community in Carroll County to its present site at Mabry Mill, milepost 176 on the Blue Ridge Parkway, near the Meadows of Dan, Virginia. It is one of the most popular stops for visitors on the Parkway.

Changing leaves and cool autumn days lured a steady stream of travelers to the

Above: Matthews Cabin shortly after it was moved and reassembled at its current location. Matthews Cabin, 1974. Courtesy National Park Service, Blue Ridge Parkway

Mary at Matthews Cabin with sweet potato custard

Parkway on those October weekends I cooked. Many came into the cabin, gathering near the warm stone hearth to see pumpkin and sweet potato pies being baked in the Dutch-oven. Blue chimney smoke, glowing embers from the hearth, a lone rocker and weaving loom, fresh mountain air and sounds from banjo players created an appealing ambience in and around the cabin. Cooking demonstrations present opportunities to share local history and heritage cooking, and so it was at the Matthews Cabin.

I will always be grateful to the Blue Ridge Parkway staff for the privilege to test my skills at the Matthews' hearth. All the pies were made with fresh local pumpkins, sweet potatoes. winesap apples, and farm eggs from the Fancy Gap community. Stone ground meal from the mill mixed with eggs, buttermilk, bacon drippings, and a touch of molasses created a delicious corn cake to accompany cranberry beans and fried sweet potatoes—truly a taste of Appalachia.

Spider frying pan

POLK MEMORIAL
PRESIDENT JAMES K. POLK STATE HISTORIC SITE
PINEVILLE, NC

t was 95 degrees the day I baked peach pies at the Polk homesite just south of Charlotte. I had been asked to present a colonial cooking workshop for the docents there.

We used fresh South Carolina peaches, sugar enough to sweeten and a basic puff paste receipt. That experience sheds light on why many early southern homes had summer kitchens.

The Polk farm is a State Memorial to honor the early childhood home of James Knox Polk, 11th President of the

United States. President Polk was born in the year 1795 on this land in Mecklenburg County, North Carolina.

While the two story log house, separate kitchen and barn is not original to the family, it does represent the kind of homestead the Polk family most likely had. Little James Polk may very well have played and worked on the grounds and creek that surround these log buildings.

The kitchen stone fireplace opening is about four feet high and of equal width, a very practical size. Prior to my arrival a staff member had thoughtfully laid the fire so that it was ready to be lit when the class began. Reproduction period pottery was stored in the cupboard and ready to use. The large table in front of the hearth was our work space for the day.

Whenever planning a cooking demonstration, I am always mindful of the season and geographic location I find myself and choose foods accordingly. This was the perfect season for peach pie.

Some of the docents peeled peaches and others took notes while we discussed cooking in the 18th century backcountry.

A puff paste is another name for pie crust.

Unbleached plain flour, a little salt, and butter were mixed well using my hands and a fork. I have had most success with the puff paste by just using my fingers to work the dough.

The two pies were baked in Dutch-ovens at the hearth and turned out beautifully. I was honored to be asked to share my

skills and knowledge with the ladies.

On another occasion I demonstrated cooking outdoors for a living history school tour. A pullet was roasted over the fire, trussed with heavy string and hung from the campfire irons. When roasting meat in this fashion it is best to position the meat to the side of the fire, not directly over it. The string can be twisted snuggly and then released so that the meat, in this case the chicken, slowly spins back and forth which works like a rotisserie. Sometimes the meat has to be repositioned to allow for even cooking. A drip pan underneath the meat catches drippings that can be used for seasoning vegetables or for making gravy or a sauce.

Corn cakes wrapped in cabbage leaves and ears of corn in the shucks were baked in hot ashes. Basic cooking like this shows what can be accomplished with little or no cooking gear.

REID HOUSE

REID PLANTATION
DENTON FARM PARK • DENTON, NC

The Southeast Old Thresher's Reunion is an annual week event held each summer at Denton Historical Park in Davidson County, North Carolina. It is the largest show of antique farm machinery in this part of the country. Visitors come by the thousands to see and explore vintage buildings, tractors, farm equipment, the steam train, threshing barn and Reid Plantation House. It has been my pleasure to cook on two occasions at the Reid hearth. Not only was it my job to share the experience of heritage cooking with visitors, but to prepare the noon meal for a group of hungry volunteers working the teams of horses at the nearby threshing barn.

My first impression of the Reid House was favorable indeed. Although it is called a plantation house it not a grand structure as many southern plantations, rather this is a practical, finely built home that holds its own elegance.

The fireplace was a good size for cooking and the chimney drew well, two things of great importance. Open windows and doors provided a gentle breeze mixed with the scents of freshly threshed wheat, sweat and lather from horses, and smoke from the steam engine. We were not without an abundance of flies. I could easily place myself in a mid-19th century farm in Piedmont North Carolina.

There was much work to be done for dinner, and thankfully there were other volunteers to help with kitchen chores: tending the fire, fetching water, shucking corn, snapping beans, making garden salad, mixing up cornbread and washing dishes. It was my duty to cut up the chickens, or young pullets for frying, which I learned by watching my mother when I was a young girl. It requires a sharp knife and steady hands. A young small chicken will bring best results. The green beans were cooked in a large pot hung over the fire from the crane and covered by a lid. A deep iron pot was used for frying the chicken and was also hung from the crane. With careful adjusting this can be done at the same time. Frying is more of a 19th century way to prepare chicken. During the morning someone cut up and mixed the garden salad and another helper prepared apples and blueberries for the cobbler. Corn was cleaned and boiled in a large pot of water. The last task was baking the corn bread and apple blueberry cobbler which required two Dutch-ovens.

The big table was laden with a platter of fried chicken, corn on the cob, green beans, tomato, cucumber, onion salad, cornbread, fruit cobbler, and two large pitchers of good water.

As we all gathered around the table and gave thanks, there was laughter and kind words. Everyone seemed to enjoy the simple farm food and it was an especially good memory for me. It took all morning, with the help of two other people, to prepare a meal for ten or so people. I had acquired a fuller understanding of a woman's life at the hearth.

SAVANNAH CABIN
FOXFIRE MUSEUM • MOUNTAIN CITY, GA

ooking at Foxfire has been a high water mark on my cooking journey. In 1972 a dear friend in Atlanta introduced me to The Foxfire Book *and I became enamored with the skills and culture of the people of Appalachia. I hold a particular fondness for the North Georgia Mountains that goes back to the days of my youth when our family camped there during summer vacations. I am intensely interested in the old ways—building log cabins, making baskets, cooking on the fireplace, quilting, and making apple butter. I held Foxfire in such high esteem for keeping these traditions. That well-used ragged book still holds a special place on my bookshelf.*

When the phone call came and I was asked to demonstrate hearth cooking for Foxfire I was ecstatic. Never did I dream that I could be a part of their program. Tears rolled down my cheeks as I sat quietly at my desk and thanked God for the blessing.

In the late 1960's, some students were challenged by their high school English teacher to document their own local heritage by interviewing older residents in the community. As a result of the popular magazine containing various articles on how to make a dulcimer, hominy, lye soap, planting by the signs, butchering hogs, and making molasses, students produced a series of books on the life, ways, and culture of the Southern Appalachians. They named it Foxfire, sometimes called "fairy fire," which is a type of fungi that grows on decaying wood and emits a bluish green light in the dark damp mountain forests.

The Foxfire Museum is located off US 441 just north of Clayton, Georgia, very close to the North Carolina state line. There are twenty log structures on the Museum grounds including a gristmill, mule barn, chapel, smoke house and wagon shed. The cabin in which I cook is the Savannah House built in 1820 by the Wilson family of Jackson County, North Carolina. It is called Savannah because that is the name of the community from which it was moved. It measures 20x20, has a large stone fireplace, a sleeping loft but no windows, and two doors facing east and west. There are two narrow openings on the cabin walls that I have been told are called loop holes. These openings are big enough to see and shoot through.

Apple pie

SAVANNAH HOUSE

On the day before each living history event I begin preparing the cabin by bringing in the kitchen box and Dutch-ovens and then starting a fire in the hearth to allow the fireplace to warm up. When a fireplace has not been used in a long while the stones get cold and damp. A fire heats up the inside walls of the hearth and chimney and chases away the dampness. Doing this prior to a cooking day provides an advantage to the cook. I have discovered that cooking in a cold fireplace takes a much longer time for baking. While the fire is going, I open the doors, let daylight in, sweep the creaking floors, fluff up the feather mattress, comfortably arrange the chairs and rocker, begin to dress the table and ask someone to bring in a bucket of well water. Then I am well on my way to a good beginning.

On the morning of the event, as the sun is taking root in the eastern sky, I make my way down to the Savannah Cabin from the volunteer guest house. The sun's rays shoot narrow beams of light down through the tall poplars and oaks. Dew is still on the grass and picket fence. Song birds break the silence and a wrap around my shoulders feels good. If I can feel a slight warmth on my palms when placing them on the hearth stones, it is a good sign.

The table I use for cooking at the hearth belonged to Aunt Arie, as did the rope bed, blanket chest and some of the other chairs in the cabin. Aunt Arie Carpenter was one of the most well known and popular

Apple Stack Cake at Foxfire

The hearth at Foxfire

persons ever interviewed by Foxfire students. She was born in the mountains near Foxfire and lived there all her life. Aunt Arie has become a role model for me. She was tough, determined, plain and worked with her hands to eke out her life and she never gave up. She did things the ways she had been taught by her "mommy and poppy."

The food dishes prepared are selected according to the season of the mountains. Most of the receipts are simple and fit appropriately into the life style of the local culture. Some include, apple stack cake, biscuits and ham, greens, brook trout, corn pones, apple pie, and roast chicken. Many receipts and ideas for foods I use come from the Foxfire book.

When I am rolling out dough for a pie on Aunt Arie's table, or washing dishes in an enamel pan on the the back porch or sweeping up crumbs, I feel like I belong to a time that no longer exists. I feel like I am home.

SNOW CAMP

ALAMANCE COUNTY, NC

The old log cabin kitchen at Snow Camp is the most primitive setting of any place I've cooked.

My initial thought upon stepping into that dark cabin with radiant beaming morning light over my shoulder was "Um, how is this going to work?" Compacted dirt floor and hearth, two wide pegged wall shelves for tables and one window. I just stood still for a moment giving my eyes and mind time to adjust.

As I began to prepare for the day it occurred to me that cooking up green pumpkins in a very simple way fit perfectly with the setting in which I

Facing: Mary and Sarah at Alamance Battleground historic site

found myself. This cabin was a likeness to early dwellings on the North Carolina frontier.

A couple of wooden bowls, skillet, knife, fork, butter and fresh pumpkins was all I needed. Visitors were amazed to see pumpkins prepared in this way, as most of us think of pumpkins only in pies.

Carefully I peeled away the tough outer skin and scooped out the seeds from the inner flesh. Then I cut the pumpkin into thin sections about one quarter inch thickness and placed them in the buttered skillet.

Pumpkin cooks quickly this way so be careful to not let the skillet get too hot causing it to burn. Turn the slices over when you see that they begin to change color. When the pumpkin is soft to the touch of a fork it is done. They may be eaten plain or strewn with a little cinnamon and sweetening on top.

Cooking that day on an earthen hearth I gained an increased awareness of frontier life. Rebecca Boone would have been right at home with me and the pumpkins.

Snow Camp is a small Quaker community settled in 1750 located in Alamance County south of Burlington, North Carolina. After the fierce Battle of Guildford Courthouse in 1781, Cornwallis and his British troops camped here to rest and regroup. It is said that during the encampment, a storm blew in and blanketed the ground with snow giving it the name Snow Camp.

G 76

SNOW CAMP

Settled by Quakers in 1749. Cornwallis camped in area after Battle of Guilford Courthouse and used home of Simon Dixon as headquarters.

TATUM CABIN
HICKORY RIDGE MUSEUM • BOONE, NC

he James and Amey Tatum cabin is a real frontier cabin with dovetail notched logs, well-trimmed hand hewn beams, oak shingles, wide plank floors and a large stone fireplace. It was built overlooking the South Fork of the New River, near Todd, about 1785, maybe earlier. One of the Tatum daughters, Sarah, married Squire Wilcoxson, a grand nephew of Daniel Boone. I wonder if Rebecca every visited this cabin?

The Tatum hearth proved to be a dandy place to try out some untested receipts from the Florida State Archives and the Metropolitan Cook Book. My cooking days took place in late fall when all the leaves had dropped and a pungent woodsy smell filled the air. Hickory and oak leaves crunched beneath my boots back and forth to the woodshed. Graciously someone always helped by fetching a pail of water.

Each day a fine fire was started to warm the stones in the chimney and hearth. When there is no constant fire going the stones in the chimney become very cold. I have learned that my baking is greatly enhanced when the stones in the hearth are warm. It is similar to preheating an oven.

Corn pudding, Cottage Bread and Mincemeat pies were all baked on the Tatum hearth and turned out beautifully. The Mincemeat was extraordinary. I wrote diary entries for these days on a piece of brown paper bag. Here are some excerpts: "Sitting at the hearth of the Tatum cabin. Fire bright autumn orange coals waiting for baking Cottage Bread, an old English style. This place is called Hickory Ridge and is in the middle of Boone. Looking out from the window there is the Coffey cabin with stone chimney. Oak and poplar logs

Cottage Bread (Receipt on page 95)

neatly stacked with dovetail notches. The ground is covered with a thick carpet of hickory leaves—brown, yellow, tan. This is indeed a stand of hickories on a ridge. Wood pile on the

porch, nicely cut and seasoned for a cook's perfect fire. Proper firewood is most important. I am alone this morning and thinking of the loveliness here. Light flows in on a breezy day, shadows fall over my writing paper and the white table cloth. I do like this cabin. The broom leaning at the doorway wall is sweet and light weight and fits me so well. I like it very much. The fireplace hearth opening is 5 feet across, 42 inches high and 3 1/2 feet deep." A perfect place to spend an autumn morning in the Blue Ridge.

Over the Campfire

REVOLUTIONARY WAR ENCAMPMENT FARE

Being part of a Revolutionary War living history regiment broadened my experience of colonial cooking over the campfire and life during the colonists' struggle for independence. Four of my ancestors served in the War of Independence and were stationed in Virginia, New England, and North Carolina. This was an opportunity to catch a glimpse of what life might have been like for them. It was both a learning and teaching experience— interacting with visitors coming through camp and learning-sharing more cooking skills from my colleagues. Sleeping in tents on the ground, fresh air, wood fires, early morning tea, sausage and apples fried in the skillet, the gentle sounds of conversation along the tent lines, the beat of drums, camaraderie with other campers, new and old friends—some of the happiest days of my life. Most of the foods prepared at the campfire for our living history regiment were simple and nutritious. Our menu depended on the growing season and the availability of food. Thinking back on those days I realize we probably ate much too well for a soldier on the move. However, we did stay true to our 18th century receipts and used that as an interpretive tool when talking with visitors. The following are some of the encampments where I cooked and the receipts used.

CORNWALLIS HOUSE
CAMDEN, SC

he Battle of Camden was a decisive engagement between Lord Cornwallis and General Gage—a humiliating and devastating defeat for the American forces. The battle occurred in August 1780 but our living history reenactment was done in November because the mid-summer heat in South Carolina is unrelenting. Fall temperatures were much more agreeable to those wearing wool uniforms or heavy frocks. Private James Bradford, a patriot ancestor in our family, was at this battle. I always felt that being there was a way to give honor to one of my grandfathers. Participants representing each side camped on the grounds and prepared meals over the campfire. It was always a pleasure to meet other reenactors in the evenings around the Cornwallis House where there would be music, dancing and light refreshments.

Some of the fare prepared in our camp at Camden included boiled ham and onions, mustard greens, lemon curd, sausage and apples, sweet potato pie, Welch rabbit, and oatmeal.

FORT DEFIANCE

CALDWELL COUNTY • LENOIR, NC

*F*ort Defiance is the home of General William Lenoir and his wife Ann. The house was completed in 1792 and takes its name from the pre-Revolutionary fortification that was situated on the tract prior to his purchase.

This was not a military fort, rather a frontier stockade erected by settlers against Indian attacks. Fort Defiance was a well-known landmark to people in the area and when Lenoir began building his home he gave it that name. The two story dwelling and meat house are the only original structures that remain. A brick floor warming kitchen in the house was used for cooking in cooler weather and also a place to keep food warm before serving in the great hall. Because of fire safety this kitchen is no longer in use. Since the original kitchen no long exists, cooking for our living history events are done outside over a fire pit. Blue mountain ridges frame in the valley of fields and woodlands along the upper Yadkin River where Fort Defiance is located. It is one of the most beautiful natural areas I have witnessed on my cooking journey and a setting that Rebecca Boone would have seen in her days here in the valley.

Cooking on an outdoor fire is a little different than working at the hearth. Although cooking is done the same way, using iron pots or Dutch-ovens, there are considerations to keep in mind such as wind, weather conditions, and fire safety. Creating enough hot coals for baking can sometimes be an issue as well. It is important to have well seasoned hard wood for creating hot coals for baking. My cooking days at the Lenoir site have been good and have turned out successes such as peach pie, pumpkin pie, stewed cushaw, persimmon pancakes, and parched corn.

On one occasion I spent two nights at the Fort which so impressed me that I penned my thoughts to paper. Here are excerpts from that entry:

"October 24, 2013. By candlelight, writing today's events at Fort Defiance in the foothills of the Blue Ridge on the head waters of the Yadkin. This morning I awoke a little before 7. A good frost covered the ground and roof. After stirring about, I dressed and made my way outside to start the day. First, I had to scrape the ice from the windshield of my truck. I needed to move it closer to my cooking spot to unload baskets and boxes. Gathering some twigs and wood shavings I started a fire that was warm and bright. Some of my fellow 18th century friends who had camped out came to the fire. At 9, school tours began. Cooking and food discussions today included peeling apples and stringing them up to dry and peeling the cushaw, cutting it into small chunks and cooking it over the fire. We made cushaw soup. Ingredients were spices, milk and a small amount of molasses. It turned out rather well. Tasters assured me it was a success. We also seeded okra, shucked corn, and collected the seeds from the cushaw for roasting. The children were delighted.

After the tours, I drove up the mountain to Boone to have supper with my granddaughter. We shopped for boots and apples and had a most delicious fare at the Daniel Boone Inn. Coming down the mountain from Blowing Rock, snow flurries and sleet pelted the windshield, but turning on to Highway 268, the sky cleared and stars shone bright in the dark county night.

When I reached the Fort I saw a candle in my little cabin window. How wonderful to find the comfort of a cozy room prepared for me—a rope bed and a feather mattress. Friday, awoke before daylight and lay in the warm covers until the dawn became more clear. After

dressing as warm as possible I moseyed over to the office to find someone was brewing coffee. Edging toward 7:30 I proceeded to start the cook fire. We soon learned that one of the schools was not coming. This gave me some extra time to browse the grounds and think. Persimmons came to mind, and to the tree I went. With delight I picked up a dozen or so plump orange fruits and made my way to my cook station. "Uhm... What should I make with persimmons?" I thought of persimmon pudding but I did not have a Dutch-oven with me. But, oh I did have a frying pan...pancakes, corncake ... yes, persimmon cakes and what a hit they made! First I took off the skins carefully and patiently put pulp and seeds in a colander and mashed the pulp with a wooden spoon. Mixed 2 eggs with persimmons and melted butter and spices. Stirred in flour and milk to get pancake consistency, spooned onto well buttered pan. They fried up perfectly. Everybody loved them. Good day."

FORT DOBBS

STATE HISTORIC SITE • STATESVILLE, NC

High on a ridge above Fourth Creek near Statesville is the site of Fort Dobbs, North Carolina's only French and Indian War connection. Built in 1756 and garrisoned by 50 Provincials under Col. Hugh Waddell, its purpose was to establish a British presence on the frontier and provide protection for settlers against Indian attacks. It was the furtherest westward British garrisoned outpost in the colonies at that time.

At one of their living history events back in the 1990s, when the site was still an obscure and mostly unnoticed place, I was asked to demonstrate

campfire cooking. In keeping with the season and time period I chose to roast a haunch of venison over a slow mellow fire. The fresh meat was soaked in a vinegar and water solution overnight. The morning of the event I arrived early to set up the campfire and cooking irons. After rubbing salt and pepper into the meat I secured the roast through the iron cross bar and laid it above the flames.

As it cooked slowly I periodically turned the meat and basted it with butter. By the end of our day the meat was done, tender and moist. It was

*delicious, and I was grateful
that it turned out so well. Many
of the living history volunteers
came by to cut off a chunk. This
is a food and cooking method
that I imagine Rebecca Boone
used many times for her large
family on the upper Yadkin.*

*The story of Fort Dobbs is
fascinating, and finally after*

*years of anticipation and plans,
reconstruction of the colonial
fortress is in the works. The
substantial structure with three
floors and a cellar will draw
visitors to the site where history
of the settlers and Cherokee on
the Carolina frontier will come
alive.*

Above: Mary loads a musket.

OLD SALEM
WINSTON SALEM, NC

A memorable, hot 4th of July living history event was in the Moravian town of Old Salem. We had been asked to come and represent the British presence in the village during the Revolution. We did this for several years but the year I remember most was camping in the apple orchard across from the Winkler Bakery. The temperature and humidity was high after musket firing demonstrations and encampment talks with visitors. The men shed their wool coats and we all settled under shade trees.

Much of the cooking was held to a minimum during that event.

We did bake a rice pudding in a Dutch-oven and although it ran over the side of the redware, it quickly disappeared and was most enjoyable. (Rice pudding can be served as a side dish or a dessert.) For breakfast we had toasted bread and cheese, cold ham and local fruit.

Old Salem is a historic district comprised of homes, businesses and gardens of the 18th century and early 19th century. The well planned

Above: Winkler Bakery

town was established in 1766 by members of the Moravian Church, a protestant group originally from the Kingdom of Moravia in eastern Europe. It is one of the most original and lovely historic spots in North Carolina.

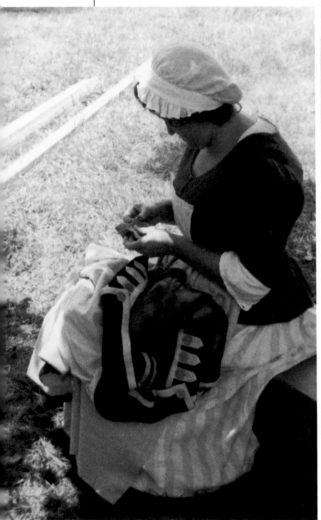

At left: Sewing on a button. Above, top to bottom: Visiting a friend. Pumpkins at Old Salem.

SURRY MUSTER FIELD
ELKIN, NC

In 2006 I was asked to do a cooking demonstration for an Overmountain Victory Trail Association (OVTA) living history school tour in Elkin and have been doing it ever since.

Our events are held in late September to commemorate the muster of the Surry Militia and their participation in The Battle of Kings Mountain on October 7, 1780. This amazing patriot victory was considered by many, including Thomas Jefferson, to be the turning point of the Revolution.

The OVTA is a friends group that supports the 330 mile Overmountain Victory National Historic Trail with preservation, protection, and interpretation endeavors.

Today our programming has grown to include public events as well as school tours. We are always situated along the national trail used by our ancestors over two centuries ago and only a short distance from the Yadkin River. My job on that first event was to show students how cooking was done on the campfire.

Arriving early in the cool fall morning, I set up the camp-fire implements and started a fire. There is something about the smell of a campfire that I like very much. That day a small hen was trussed with cord and hung to the side of the fire for roasting. Corn pones were cooked in a cast iron pot hung from the cross bar of the fire irons. Both students and teachers were in awe of cooking a chicken in that fashion and seeing the cornbread made into little cakes.

Through the years I have used a variety of receipts at these events representing possible foods the men and their families might have had here in the Yadkin Valley. Those include baked butternut squash, boiled turnips, stewed pumpkin, venison, apple pie, and fried bacon and ham.

Cooking for the students in this location is especially meaningful to me as this is the area in which I call home. Many of the men who served in the local Surry and Wilkes Militias at the Battle Kings Mountain lived here and are buried in old church or family cemeteries. My local history truly is American History.

M 53

SURRY MUSTER FIELD

Patriot militia, led by Major Joseph Winston, gathered in this vicinity, Sept. 1780, marched to victory at Kings Mtn.

NORTH CAROLINA OFFICE OF ARCHIVES AND HISTORY   2003

TANNENBAUM PARK

GUILFORD COURT HOUSE • GREENSBORO, NC

arch 15, 1780 was the date of the large and bloody battle between General Nathaniel Greene and Lord Cornwallis at a place in North Greensboro, called Guilford Court House. Although the British held the field, they suffered greatly and when reports reached London, Charles Fox, a member of Parliament said, "Another such victory would ruin the British Army." Today the Battlefield is a National Military Park.

When we camped at Tannenbaum Park near the Hoskins House, there were always large crowds that came to see the British and American encampments. It was rewarding to be able to share cooking history of the era. The first meal I cooked at Guilford was a stew of beef with carrots, potatoes, and onions. Often the fare for breakfast was oatmeal and sausages with cheese and bread. Egg and Bacon Pie was also a favorite.

Above: Hoskins House at Tannenbaum Park

COLONIAL WILLIAMSBURG

Chowning's Tavern

PALACE GREEN
COLONIAL WILLIAMSBURG, VA

Camping on the green in front of the historic Governors' Palace in Williamsburg was a reenactor's dream. The Labor Day weekend living history event was one of the most coveted of the year and we considered it a great honor to be asked to attend. Our unit along with others were set up in long rows of white tents with a dining fly and officers marque. Participants outfitted in period dress walked the grounds against the back drop of Burton Church, the George Wythe house, picket fences, Greenhow Store, colonial gardens and horse drawn carriages. Visitors mingled in camp falling into conversations with the soldiers, and becoming immersed with the women at the campfire and cook table under the dining fly. It was here that I found a deep sense of accomplishment and pride to share colonial cooking skills with those who seemed so eager to learn.

Many of the visitors at Williamsburg were internationals

Above: A view along Duke of Gloucester Street

and families from across the country who had come to catch a glimpse of colonial America. For those few days we were the face of Williamsburg.

In the early dawn just as the birds begin to chirp and the distant rooster announced it was a new day, the camp was quiet, colored by a soft mist rising from the earth. Many times I put the kettle over the new fire preparing breakfast for our unit. In late evening all of us would gather for supper by candle light. At dusk dampness fell into the air and the warmth of the campfire lured both reenactors and lingering guests. For a beautiful moment we were in the 18th century.

Welch Rabbit, boiled ham, roast beef and potatoes, corn, fresh fruit, sausage and oatmeal, bread, fried ham, and pork pie were some of the dishes I prepared for our Williamsburg encampment.

· ·

Top: At the Regimental Dinner on the Green. Left: Campfire pies. Facing: Garden party at the Governor's Palace

COOKING TEMPERATURES

Today's cooks rely on temperature gauges. Colonial cooks learned from trial and error and could estimate the temperature of a Dutch-oven with great skill. What one cook would describe as a "fast" oven, another may have described as "moderate." Today, the descriptions of these terms vary, depending on the source, but not usually by more than 25 degrees.

Slack oven: moderately warm

Very slow / very low oven: 300-325° F.

Slow / low oven: 325-350° F.

Moderate / medium oven: 350-375° F.

Fast / quick / high oven: 375-400° F.

Very fast / very quick / very high oven: 400-425° F.

Colonial Receipts

*Prepared by Mary Bohlen at
the Hearth and over the Campfire*

As much as possible, receipts are shown in their original form, complete with misspellings and language common to the era. Clarifications are added. Modern recipes follow some of the original receipts to assist today's cook.

"HERBS USEFUL IN COOKERY

Thyme, is good for soups and stuffings.

Sweet Marjoram, is used in Turkeys.

Summer Savory, ditto, and in Sausages and salted Beef, and legs of Pork.

Sage, is used in Cheese and Pork, but not generally approved.

Parsley, good in soups, and to garnish roast Beef, excellent with bread and butter in the Spring.

Penny Royal, is a high aromatic, altho' a spontaneous herb in old ploughed fields, yet might be more generally cultivated in gardens, and used in cookery and medicines.

Sweet Thyme, is most useful and best approved in cookery."

Amelia Simmons, *The First American Cookbook, A Facsimile of "American Cookery,"* 1796.

BREADS

"Give us this day our daily bread."

It would be hard to imagine life without bread. It is so much a part of our life that we may not even think about how precious a commodity it was for people centuries ago. Today we can go to the supermarket and purchase a loaf of bread or a bag of flour with no thought of how it got to the grocery shelf. In the years before modern bakeries farm families depended on a good wheat harvest, community threshing parties, and a good cook fire in order to have a fresh loaf on the table. What could be better for a hungry stomach than some warm bread and butter with a little molasses or jam?

HEARTH BREAD - *For Today's Cook*

1 pkg. dry yeast
1/3 c. sugar (or 4 Tbsp. of honey)
1/3 c. oil or butter
1 ½ c. hot water
2 tsp. salt
5-6 c. bread flour

Mix 4 cups flour with dry yeast. Dissolve sugar, salt, and oil in very warm water. When mixed, combine with flour and yeast mixing well. Gradually add more flour until dough is elastic and smooth. Knead for about five minutes. Place dough in a large bowl that has been lightly coated with oil or butter. This will prevent sticking. Cover with cloth and place in a warm spot until dough rises double. Punch down dough and knead for another five minutes. Form into 2 round loaves and put into greased pans that will be later placed in Dutch-ovens. (Two Dutch-ovens will be needed, or bake one loaf at a time.) Allow dough to rise double again. While dough is rising, preheat Dutch-ovens near fire, but do not get too hot. When loaves are ready, set Dutch-oven directly over a small mound of hot coals that have been shoveled onto the hearth. Place loaf into oven and cover with lid. Shovel hot coals on top. Bake until done. More coals may need to be added to maintain heat for baking. Loaf is ready when it sounds hollow when tapped. This recipe works well for both hearth cooking and in modern ovens.

Note: This recipe is one I have baked both on the hearth and in my kitchen. It is similar to a Penny Loaf receipt used at the historic Van Cortlandt Manor Kitchen in Westchester County, New York where, interestingly, some of my ancestors settled.

Penny loaf and half penny roles

A penny loaf was a common size loaf of bread in England during the 1700s and before. Up until the beginning of the 19th century the size, weight, and ingredients of bread sold in the market place was regulated by the The Assize of Bread Act of 1266. The actual cost and weight of a loaf varied depending on the kind of flour used and fluctuation of the price of corn (wheat). When the price of wheat rose the size of the loaf was smaller. If the price of wheat lowered the loaf was bigger. The weights of the loaves differed according to three classes of flour; finely bolted, wheaten made from more coarse flour, and unbolted wheat much like our whole wheat flour. The latter loaf would have weighed more because of the sifted wheat. Bakers could be fined if it was found that they sold loaves that were not of full measure.

A penny loaf cost one old penny which was worth 1/240 of a pound of sterling. This was a time when there were 240 pence in a pound. Twelve pence made a shilling and 20 shillings made a pound, hence 240 pence in a pound.

A halfpenny was an English coin that was half the value of an old penny. Halfpenny roles were smaller than the penny loaf. Many of the old English cookbooks mention penny loaf bread.

ORDINARY BREAD

This receipt is from *The Backcountry Housewife*, a wonderful and resourceful cookbook published by the Schiele Museum in Gastonia, North Carolina. It is a good basic bread recipe for learning the art of baking on the hearth. Makes one loaf.

    3 c. unbleached flour
    ½ tsp. salt
    ¼ oz. yeast
    1 c. warm water

Mix salt and flour well. Dissolve yeast into water. Add to flour. Mix well and form into a ball. Add more flour if too moist. Cover and let rise until doubled (about 2 hours). Knock down dough and knead well. Form into the shape of a ball and place in pan to be used in Dutch-oven. Cover and place in a warm spot for the second rising. Allow dough to rise double. Bake in hot oven.

COTTAGE BREAD

"1 qt of flour, 1 table spoon full of sugar, 1 [indecipherable] of butter, 1 egg, [indecipherable] tea cup of yeast, make it up of milk or water very soft & put it aside to rise."

Handwritten script in a notebook, Florida State Archives.

Notes from the Cook regarding Cottage Bread:

This is a hearty traditional English bread that dates to the mid nineteenth century and probably much earlier. There are two ways I have baked Cottage Bread at the Tatum hearth in Boone. My first experience was making a single round loaf in the Dutch-oven. The other was two round loaves; a regular round loaf on the bottom and a smaller round loaf on top. For this, baking must be done in a deep Dutch-oven to allow for the height of the bread, or in a brick oven. It is thought that baking a double layer loaf in this fashion allowed more space for other loaves in the oven.

For Today's Cook:

> 1 qt. unbleached bread flour
> 1 tsp. salt
> 1 Tbsp. sugar
> 1 Tbsp. butter
> 1 egg
> 2 tsp. (or one package) fast-rising yeast
> 1 and 1/3 c. lukewarm water or milk.

Preheat oven to 375° and bake for about one hour or until loaf sounds hollow when tapped.

TO MAKE A SCOTCH-RABBIT

"Toast a Piece of Bread very nicely on both Sides, butter it, cut a Slice of Cheese, about as big as the Bread, toast it on both sides, and lay it on the Bread."

Hannah Glasse. *The Art of Cookery Made Plain and Easy,* 1747.

TO MAKE A WELCH-RABBIT

"Toast the Bread on both Sides, then toast the Cheese on one Side, and lay it on the Toast, and with a hot Iron brown the other Side. You may rub it over with Mustard."

Hannah Glasse. *The Art of Cookery Made Plain and Easy*, 1747.

TO MAKE AN ENGLISH-RABBIT

"Toast a Slice of Bread brown on both Sides, then lay it in a Plate before the Fire, pour a Glass of Red Wine over it, and let it soak the Wine up; then cut some Cheese very thin, and lay it very thick over the Bread; put it in a Tin Oven before the Fire, and it will be toasted and brown presently. Serve it away hot." (Can be browned in a Dutch-oven.)

Hannah Glasse. *The Art of Cookery Made Plain and Easy*, 1747.

ROLLS

"Warm 2 ounces of butter in a pint of milk and put in it two spoonsful of yeast and a little salt. Add two pounds of flour and let it rise an hour. Knead it well and make it into rolls. Bake in a quick oven."

Original receipt from [James] Monroe Family Recipes. College of William and Mary. Ash Lawn-Highland, Charlottesville, Virginia. 1988.

ROLLS – *For Today's Cook*

Baked in the beehive oven at Latta Plantation's reproduction kitchen.

2 Tbsp. butter
1 c. milk
1 package dry yeast
1 tsp. salt
4 c. flour

Instructions continue on next page.

Heat the milk with the butter, stirring to melt the butter. Remove milk from heat. Cool to lukewarm and add the yeast. Let mixture sit for five minutes. Stir in salt and flour. Knead the dough for five minutes. Cover and let it rise for one hour in a warm place. Punch down the dough and knead it again for five minutes. Shape into small rolls on ungreased baking sheets. Cover and let rise for about an hour. Bake rolls for 20 minutes at 350°. Makes 18 rolls.

PLAIN BISCUIT – Officers' & Common Fare

2 c. plain unbleached flour
1 oz. butter
1 egg
½ c. milk

Into a bowl put milk and melted butter. Add egg and 1 cup of flour. Mix well. Continue to add flour until a bread-like consistency is formed. Knead until dough is soft. Break into small pieces about the size of a large egg and roll into a ball. Place in baking pan and press biscuits gently to flatten. You may also roll out dough and use biscuit cutter. Bake 10-12 mins in 350° or until lightly browned. For more modern tastes, add 1/2 tsp of baking powder to help the biscuits rise. Works well in Dutch-oven.

Cooked at Latta Plantation and Allen Kitchen. Recipe is an adaptation from Amelia Simmon's *American Cookery* taken from *The King's Bread, 2d Rising.*

CRACKERS FOR THE SICK

"One pound of flour, one egg, not beaten, one tablespoon of yeast; one tablespoon of cream, a little salt; mix all together with milk to a stiff paste, and beat them twenty minutes with a rolling pin, to be rolled in small round pieces, separately, very thin. [Bake.]"   From General William Lenoir Papers, Fort Defiance, Lenoir, NC.

DELICIOUS CORN BREAD — *Mrs. Wilcox*

"Stir a quart of boiling milk into a pint of yellow corn meal, add to it a tea cupful of molasses and three or four well beaten eggs, a tea spoonful of salt, then pour it into a buttered basin; bake in a moderate oven for two hours. Or add to this mixture, a table spoon of sweet butter, butter saucers, half fill them and bake half an hour in a quick oven."   Florida State Archives. Handwritten script in a notebook.

MARY EVA'S CORNBREAD (Spider Cornbread)

This is an adaptation from *Tullie's Receipts* cookbook of the Atlanta Historical Society.

> 2 c. stone ground cornmeal. If the meal is too course,
>   use ½ c. flour with 1½ c. cornmeal.
> 1 tsp. salt
> 2 Tbsp. bacon grease
> 1½ cups buttermilk or enough to make a stiff batter
> 1 egg (optional)

Bake in a preheated Dutch-oven for open hearth cooking method. Preheat a modern oven at 400 or 425° and bake for 25-30 minutes. Corn pones can be made by dropping spoonfuls in a skillet over medium fire and then turning to brown on other side. Mix dry ingredients, bacon grease, and buttermilk. The batter should be stiff. Pour into a pan and bake.

Note: This will be a hearty bread with a heavier texture because it is made with plain meal. Spider cornbread is a name derived by the practice of baking cornbread in a skillet that was called a spider—so named because the heavy three-legged black pan had a long handle and resembled the shape of a spider.

INDIAN SLAPJACK

"One quart of milk, 1 pint of Indian meal, 4 eggs, 4 spoons of flour, little salt, beat together, baked on girdles (griddles), or fry in a dry pan, or baked in a pan which has been rub'd with suet, lard or butter."
Amelia Simmons, The First American Cookbook

INDIAN SLAPJACK – *For Today's Cook*

1 c. milk
1 egg
½ c. plain cornmeal
¼ c. flour
a pinch of salt

Mix corn meal, flour and salt. Add beaten egg and milk. Cook as you would small pancakes. Makes 12 cakes.

JOHNY (Johnny) CAKE, or HOE CAKE

"Scald 1 pint of milk and put to 3 pints of Indian meal, and half pint of flower (flour)—bake before a fire. Or scald with milk two thirds of the Indian meal, or wet two thirds with boiling water, add salt, molasses and shortening, work up with cold water pretty stiff, and bake as above."
Amelia Simmons, The First American Cookbook

SALADS

Sallet, sallade, and salad all come from the Latin *salata* (salty), meaning salted herbs such as raw vegetables with dressing of oil and/or vinegar. The term *sallet* first appears in the English language in the 14th century.

Receipts for salads scarcely show up in early American cookbooks, however there are references in old world accounts and manuscripts that give us an idea of what a salad consisted of for our ancestors.

In his book *Acetaria, A Discourse of Sallets* published in London, 1699, John Evelyn wrote "Sallets in general consist of certain esculent [edible] plants and herbs....of several kinds to be eaten raw or green, blanched, or candid; simple and perse [by itself] or intermingled with others according to the season....eaten with some acetous juice, oyl, [oil] salt, etc. to give them a grateful gust and vehicle."

Lettuce of all sorts, greens, cucumbers, celery, carrots, leeks, radishes, turnips, spinach, beets, onions and cabbage were used in salads. From local Moravian garden records we know that all of these were being grown in the Yadkin Valley where the Bryans and Boones lived.

In colonial times not only would cooks use these garden vegetables but an assortment of wild greens could be foraged as well, such as dock, chickweed, dandelion, sorrel, and creasy greens. Frontier women like Rebecca may have used wild greens as a supplement in fresh salads or stews.

Salt and vinegar were used for dressings along with black pepper and oil, if available. It is interesting to note that the Moravians wrote about using bear oil as a replacement for imported oil.

Note: When gathering wild foods be sure you know your selection is safe and edible and that the fields and meadows are free of pesticides and other contaminants.

TO DRESS A SALAD

"After you have duly proportioned the Herbs, take two thirds of Oil of Olives, one third of Vinegar, some hard Eggs cut small, both the Whites and Yolks, a little Salt and some Mustard, all which must be well-mixed, and poured over the Sallad, having first cut the large Herbs, such as Celery, Endive, Cabbage-Lettuce, but none of the small ones: Then mix all well together, that it may be ready just when you want to use it, for the Oil will make it presently soften and lose its briskness."

Adam's Luxury and Eve's Cookery, 1744

SIMPLE SALAD DRESSING - *Traditional*

3 parts pure olive oil
1 part wine, apple cider vinegar, or fresh lemon juice
salt and pepper to taste
fresh herbs

For best results, use virgin olive oil. Do not use ready-flavored vinegars. Make dressing fresh each time. It can be mixed in a glass or pottery cup. Add salt, pepper, and herbs to the oil and vinegar, and then toss the greens with the dressing.

Olive oil was an imported product and may not have been available in the Carolina backcountry. Salads could be prepared using bear oil or no oil at all.

CHICKWEED SALAD - *Traditional*

Chickweed is a wild green that gets its name from the fact that chickens love to eat it and it also helps them produce more eggs. Chickweed is an excellent addition to salads and soups and can also be cooked as a pot herb or made into tea. Chickweed should be cooked very lightly since overcooking depletes its nutritional value.

chickweed
light olive oil
lemon juice or vinegar

Gather fresh chickweed, cutting or breaking off the tender tops away from the ground. Wash well and drain. Add small amounts of olive oil, lemon juice, and salt and pepper to taste. A zingy spring dish!

DANDELION SALAD - *Traditional*

The word "dandelion" comes from the French word "dent-de-lion," meaning "tooth of the lion." The name of this spring green comes from the pointed edges of its leaves which resemble rows of teeth. Dandelion leaves are a good source of vitamin A and can be made into salads or cooked as greens. Gather only tender young leaves.

tender young dandelion leaves
other salad greens such as lettuces, beet tops, spinach, or
    chickweed can be added
salt (to soak leaves)
1 clove garlic sliced in half (optional)
3-4 slices of bacon

Wash leaves well and drain. Then soak leaves in cold salty water for only a few minutes to help draw out bitterness. Drain and dry with a clean towel and set aside.

Take half a clove of garlic and rub the inside of the salad bowl well.

Cut bacon strips into small pieces and cook in skillet over medium heat until crispy. Remove from heat and stir red wine vinegar quickly into skillet, mixing bacon drippings with the vinegar. Pour vinegar mixture over salad and serve.

If bacon produces too much grease, pour some out before mixing in the vinegar.

Garnish with chopped or sliced boiled eggs if desired.

MEAT & MAIN DISHES

Beef

TO BOYLE [Boil] A RUMPE OF BEEFE

"Take a rumpe of beefe, beeing clean washed, & put it into a good deale of water in a stone pot, then take a quarter of a peck of pot hearbs shread small & put them into ye beefe. when it is seasoned with salt to your likeing, allsoe put in 2 or 3 shread ounions. & when it hath boyled an houre & halfe leasurely, cut 6 carrets in quarters & put into it, & a spoonfull of whole pepper. soe let it stew 5 or 6 houres, then serve it up with sippets and as much liquor poured on it as ye dish will hould. but before you take it up, season it to yr taste [with white] wine vinegar & let it have but one boyle after."

Martha Washington, *Martha Washington's Booke of Cookery and Booke of Sweetmeats* Transcribed by Karen Hess. (New York: Columbia University Press, 1981).

Note: Pot herbs are leafy green vegetables. A sippet is a small piece of bread or toast used for dipping. Liquor refers to drippings.

TO STEW A RUMP IN A PLAIN MANNER WITH ROOTS

"Brown and put in pot of boiling water; after boiling an hour, put in some carrots, turnips and onions. When near ready, make a sauce thus: Brown a ¼ pound of butter and thicken with flour, mix it into a choppin of your soup, give it a boil, put in a spoonful of ketchup, and scum it. Dish up rump, and pour sauce over it and garnish it with the boiled carrot and turnip. Then serve up your soup by itself on toasts of bread."

Mrs. Frazer, *The Practice of Cookery, Pastry, Pickling, Preserving, &c.*, 1791.

Note: A choppin is an old Scottish unit of measure, about a quart. Ketchup in this receipt refers to a mushroom sauce, not what we think of today as a tomato based sauce. To scum is to remove a layer of foam.

TO MAKE A COMMON MINCED PIE

"Parboil 3 pounds of tender beef; when it is cold mince it with ½ pound suet, stone and minced 3½ pounds of raisins, ½ dozen apples cut small, 1 pound of currants cleaned and picked, add to these the grate of a lemon, ½ ounce Jamaica pepper, a few cloves, and a nutmeg, all beat together and mixed with 2 teaspoons salt. Put all together in a bowl and moisten with ½ mutchkin of the gravy the meat was boiled in, and a gill of white wine. Cover your pan with a standing paste; then put in your meat, and cover it with a puff'd paste."

Mrs. Frazer, *The Practice of Cookery, Pastry, Pickling, Preserving, &c.*, 1791.

Note: A gill is equal to ¼ pint. A mutchkin is a Scottish measurement equal to ¾ pint. (See Puff'd Paste receipt, page 136.)

MINCED PIE OF BEEF

"Four pound boiled beef, chopped fine, and salted; six pound of raw apple chopped also, one pound beet suet, one quart of wine of rich sweet cider, one ounce mace, and cinnamon, a nutmeg, two pounds raisins, bake in paste [pastry], three fourths of an hour.

Observations: All meat pies require a hotter and brisker oven than fruit pies. In good cookeries, all raisins should be stoned. As people differ in their tastes, they may alter to their wishes. And as it is difficult to ascertain with precision the small articles of spicery; everyone may relish as they like, and suit their taste."

Amelia Simmons, *The First American Cookbook*, 1796.

Roasting Fowl

Together, the two following receipts explain how a small fowl is roasted in a fireplace or on a campfire. To truss means tie up the wings and legs of the bird. It is hung low, near the fire and the string twisted frequently so that the bird rotates much like a rotisserie and browns on all sides. The bird could also be attached to a spit in front of the fire. Be careful to not get the bird too close to the flames. Drippings can be caught in a tray or some other container and used to baste the bird or later made into gravy. It usually takes longer to cook than noted in these receipts. Estimated cooking time is about 3 hours. Cooking time may vary depending on the heat of the coals.

ROASTING ON A STRING: "TO ROAST PIGEONS"

"Take some parsley shred fine, a piece of butter as big as a walnut, a little pepper and salt; tie the neck end tight: tie a string round the legs and rump, and fasten the other end to the top of the chimney-piece: Baste them with butter, and when they are enough, lay them in the dish, and they will swim with gravy. Twenty minutes will roast them."

Hannah Glasse, *The Art of Cookery Made Plain and Easy*, 1747.

TO ROAST YOUNG CHICKENS

"When you kill young chickens, pluck them very carefully, truss and put them down to a good fire, dredge and baste them with lard: they will take a quarter of an hour in roasting: froth them up, lay them on the dish, pour butter and parsley on and send them up hot."

Mary Randolph, *The Virginia Housewife* or, *Methodical Cook; a facsimile of an authentic early American cookbook.*

DIRECTIONS FOR ROASTING A GOOSE

"Take some sage, wash and pick it clean, and an onion; chop them very fine, with some pepper and salt, and put them into the belly; let your goose be clean picked, and wiped dry with a dry cloth, inside and out; one hour will roast a large goose, three quarters of an hour, a small one. Serve it in your dish with some brown gravy, applesauce in a boat, and some gravy in another."

Hannah Glasse, *The Art of Cookery Made Plain and Easy,* 1747.

PRUNE SAUCE FOR LAND FOWL

"1 lb. prunes, 21 fl. oz. water, ½ tsp. ground ginger, ½ tsp. cinnamon, 2 oz. sugar. Simmer the prunes in the water for about one hour until tender. Cool, then remove the stones. Boil the prunes and the juice about ¼ pint with the ginger, cinnamon and sugar for about 2-3 minutes, until thick, stirring constantly. Serve with chicken, turkey, duck or goose.

Note: This rich sauce may be used as a black tart filling."

John Nott, *The Cooks and Confectioners Dictionary,* 1726.

ROAST CHICKEN WITH LEMON BALM - *Traditional*

This dish can be made in a Dutch-oven at the hearth. Note: frontier cooks may not have had access to lemons or imported ginger root.

small roasting chicken, about 4 lbs.
1 tsp. salt
3 Tbsp. lemon juice (optional)
1 inch long piece of peeled ginger root (optional)
15 sprigs of lemon balm, 4–5 inches long
fresh lemon balm sprigs, for garnish

Rinse chicken and pat dry. Dissolve salt in lemon juice, and rub chicken inside and out. Use ginger and half of the lemon balm sprigs to rub chicken, and then stuff the chicken with them. Place the chicken, breast side up, in an oiled roasting pan. Cover with the rest of the lemon balm sprigs. Roast at 375° for about 1 hour, or until done. Remove herbs from inside the chicken, and place the chicken on a serving platter. Let cool for about 10 minutes, garnish with fresh lemon balm and serve.

Receipt from James K. Polk Historic Site. Charlotte, NC.

Fish

TO ROAST A SHAD
Based on a receipt from *The Virginia Housewife, 1824* and notes from *The Backcountry Housewife* (Schiele Museum, 1985).

1 large shad or other fish
bacon strips (optional)
bread crumbs
salt and pepper, to taste
melted butter
hardwood plank a little longer than the fish
cord or string

Clean the fish well. Cover with bread crumbs. Grease plank and place fish on it. Place bacon strips across fish at top and bottom, and attach the fish securely to the board with cord or string. Season fish with salt, pepper, and crumbs, then drizzle with melted butter. Prop plank at an angle before the fire to roast it, outward and away from the hot coals of a hearth fire or campfire.

If you want to save the juices, place a drip pan at the bottom of the plank. Bake about 30 minutes, or until the flesh flakes easily off when touched with a fork or knife. Cooking time may vary depending on the heat of the coals.

Lamb

TO MAKE MINCED PIES OF MUTTON

"Take a leg of mutton, four pound of beef-suet, bone the leg, and cut it raw into small pieces, as also the suet, mince them together very fine, and being minced season it with two pound of currans [currants], two pound of raisins, 2 pound of prunes, an ounce of caraway-seed, an ounce of nutmegs, an ounce of pepper, an ounce of cloves and mace and six ounces of salt; stir up all together, fill the pies and bake them as the former."

Robert May, *The Accomplisht Cook*, 1671.

For Today's Cook:

    1 lb. very lean boneless leg of lamb or lamb steak, ground
    1/2 lb. beef kidney suet, ground
    1 c. currants
    1 c. raisins
    3/4 c. pitted and quartered prunes
    1/2 tsp. each: caraway seeds, ground cloves, mace,
        freshly ground nutmeg and black pepper
    2 tsp. salt
    Pastry crust (see following recipe)

Note: beef and beef suet can be substituted for lamb and kidney.

Preheat oven to 350°.

In a large bowl combine all ingredients blending very well with your hands. Set aside or place in refrigerator until needed. Prepare pastry crust. Pat the dough in the bottom and sides of a baking pan.

Fill the pastry with the minced meat and place dough lid on top. Crimp edges together. Make a small hole in the center of the pie dough to allow steam to escape. Left over pastry dough can be used to make cut outs for the top of the pie. Bake for 1½ hours.

Allow pie to set for one hour before removing from pan. Spread icing when pan is cooled.

PASTRY CRUST AND ICING

"Fill your pies, close them up, bake them and being baked, ice them with double refined sugar, rose water, and butter. Make the paste with a peck of flour and two pound of butter boild in fair water....Make it up boiling hot...." Robert May, *The Accomplisht Cook*, 1671.

Pastry Crust:
    ½ lb. butter
    ½ c. water
    4 c. flour
    ½ tsp. salt
    2 Tbsp. sugar

Combine butter and water in saucepan and bring to a boil. Stir until butter dissolves. In a large bowl mix the flour, salt, and sugar. Make a well in the flour and slowly pour liquid into it stirring constantly with a fork. Knead the dough gently until it is firm and forms a ball.

Take about one third of the dough for the crust and wrap in a towel and set in a warm place. Quickly roll out the remaining dough to about ½ inch thickness and place in baking dish. Roll out the top crust as soon as the pie is filled and fit into place.

Pastry Icing:
    2 Tbsp. butter at room temperature
    5 Tbsp. confectioners' sugar
    ½ tsp. rose water

Mix all ingredients well. Spread on cooled pie. Serve warm or at room temperature

Note: This pie will have a slightly thick crust and may be crunchy. Because of its dense nature the pie can be removed from the baking dish and served on a platter. It is not likely that Rebecca Boone would have had a pie exactly like this on the frontier simply because of the cost and difficulty of getting the imported ingredients. She could, however, have made a minced pie using her own ingenuity substituting ingredients.

This receipt gives us an example of the differences of food choices in the back settlements compared to dining in Williamsburg, Charleston, or London.

Pork

TO MAKE A CHESHIRE PORK PIE FOR SEA

"Take some salt pork that has been boiled, cut it into thin slices, an equal quantity of potatoes pared and sliced thin, make a good crust, cover the dish, lay a layer of meat seasoned with a little pepper, and a layer of potatoes, then a layer of meat, a layer of potatoes, and so on till your pie is full; season it with pepper when it is full, lay some butter on top, then fill your dish above half full of soft water; close your pie up, and bake it in a gentle oven."

Hannah Glasse, *The Art of Cookery Made Plain and Easy*, 1747.

PICKLED PORK

"After washing and scraping it perfectly clean, put it into the pot with water cold, and when the rind feels tender, it is enough. The general sauce is greens, among the variety which you are to make choice to your own direction."

William Henderson, *The Housekeeper's Instructor*, 1795.

Note: Pickled and Salt Pork are the same (same goes for beef). Also, bacon in the 18th century meant any salted pork, including ham, not just side-meat. By the same token, salt pork is not the same as fatback, but refers to the meat.

FRIED SAUSAGES

"Take half a pound of sausages, and six apples, slice four about as thick as a crown, cut the other two in quarters, fry them with the sausages of fine light brown, lay the sausages in the middle of the dish, and the apples round. Garnish with the quartered apples. Stewed cabbage and sausages fried is a good dish."

Hannah Glasse, *The Art of Cookery Made Plain and Easy*, 1747.

Note: A crown is a British coin equal to five shillings.

Venison

VENISON STEW - *for today's cook, based on Mrs. Frazier's receipt*

The Bryan-Boone family were hunters who would have provided a steady supply of meat for the table.

Other game like elk, bear, or squirrel could have been used as well, along with whatever vegetables or herbs were available. Rebecca most likely cooked stews in a big open kettle and increased the quantities of ingredients to feed her large family.

For marinating:
    1 onion, sliced
    venison roast or venison cut up for stew, about 2½ pounds
    apple cider vinegar, about one quart

For stew:

  2-3 medium onions
  4 carrots
  2–3 turnips
  1 medium cabbage quartered
  4 medium potatoes
  salt and pepper, to taste

Place venison and slices of onion in a pottery crock or large bowl. Cover completely with apple cider vinegar and let marinate in refrigerator for 2 days.

Remove meat from container and wash well in cold water. Put in a large pot of water and quickly bring to a boil, then reduce heat and cook until meat is tender. Remove meat and cut into small pieces. Add chopped vegetables to broth and cook until tender. Return meat to cooking pot and thicken the broth with 4 or 5 table-spoons of flour or freshly grated bread crumbs. Salt and pepper to taste.

VEGETABLES & SIDE DISHES

"The best cook cannot alter the first quality, they must be good, or the cook will be disappointed."
—Amelia Simmons, *The First American Cookbook*

TO BOIL ALL KINDS OF GARDEN STUFF

"In dressing all sorts of garden herbs, take care they are clean washed; that there be no small snails, or caterpillars between the leaves; and that all the coarse outer leaves, and the tops that have received any injury by the weather, be taken off. Next wash them in a good deal of water, and put them into a cullender [colander] to drain. Care must likewise be taken, that your pot or sauce-pan be clean, well tinned, and free from sand, or grease."

Susannah Carter, *The Frugal Housewife* or, *Complete Woman Cook; The American Antiquarian Cookbook Collection*. (Kansas City, Missouri: Andrews McMeel Publishing, LLC, 2013).

TO MAKE AN ONION PIE

"Wash and pare some potatoes and cut them in slices, peel some onions, cut them in slices, pare some apples and slice them, make a good crust, cover your dish, lay a quarter of a pound of butter all over, take a quarter of an ounce of mace beat fine, a nutmeg grated, a tea-spoonful of beaten pepper, three tea-spoonfuls of salt; mix all together, strew some over the butter, lay a layer of potatoes, a layer of onions, a layer of apples, and a layer of eggs [boiled], and so on till you have filled your pie, strewing a little of the seasoning between each layer, and a quarter of a pound of butter in bits, and six spoonfuls of water; close your pie, and bake it an hour and a half. A pound of potatoes, a pound of onions, a pound of apples, and twelve eggs will do."

Hannah Glasse, *The Art of Cookery Made Plain and Easy*, 1747

Pumpkin & Squash

POMPKIN

"One quart of milk, 1 pint pumpkin, 4 eggs, molasses, allspice and ginger in a crust, make a hour."

Amelia Simmons, *The First American Cookbook, A Facsimile of "American Cookery,"* 1796.

Note: maple syrup, honey, or sugar can be used in place of molasses. Sweeten to taste.

POTATO PUMPKIN

"Get one of good colour and seven or eight inches in diameter; cut a piece of the top, take out all the seeds, wash and wipe the cavity, pare the rind off, and fill the hollow with good forcemeat, put the top on and set it in a deep pan to protect the sides; bake it in a moderate oven, put it carefully in the dish without breaking, and it will look like a handsome mould. Another way of cooking potato pumpkin is to cut it in slices, pare off the rind and make a puree."

Randolph, *The Virginia Housewife*, 1824.

Note: Forcemeat is derived from the French "farcir" meaning to stuff. A mixture of meat or vegetables/fruit chopped and seasoned for stuffing.

For Today's Cook:

Make forcemeat with pork, veal, suet or sausage. Brown with onions. Measure ingredients according to the size of forcemeat needed for pumpkin. Add to browned meat, pieces of bread, one or two eggs, chopped apples, parsley, thyme, cinnamon, nutmeg, mace and grated lemon rind to taste.

BAKED WHOLE PUMPKIN - *Traditional*
    1 pumpkin, 5-7 lb.
    6 whole eggs
    2 c. whipping cream
    ½ c. brown sugar
    1 Tbsp. molasses
    ½ tsp. nutmeg
    1 tsp. cinnamon
    ¼ tsp. ginger
    2 Tbsp. butter

Wash pumpkin well and dry. Cut a piece from the top, take out all the seeds, wash and wipe the cavity out but don't remove peel. Mix all the ingredients except the butter. Fill the pumpkin and top with butter. Cover the pumpkin and bake at 350° for 1½ hours until set like custard. Serve from the pumpkin, scraping some of the pumpkin off with each serving.

Watauga County Recipes: a taste of Appalachia (Boone, NC: Watauga County Extension Homemakers, 1999).

SQUASH OR CIMLIN [Simlin]

"Gather young squashes, peel, and cut them in two; take out the seeds, and boil them till tender; put them into a colander, drain off the water, and rub them with a wooden spoon through the colander; then put them onto a stew-pan, with a cupful of cream, a small piece of butter, some pepper and salt, stew them, stirring very frequently until dry. This is the most delicate way of preparing squashes."

Mary Randolph, *The Virginia Housewife or, Methodical Cook; a facsimile of an authentic early American cookbook*

WINTER SQUASH

"The crooked neck of this squash is the best part. Cut it in close to an inch thick, take off the rind, and boil them with salt in the water; drain them well before they are dished, and pour melted butter over—serve them up very hot.

The large part, containing the seeds, must be sliced and pared, cut it in small pieces and stew it till soft, with just water enough to cover it, pass it through a sieve and stew it again, adding some butter, pepper, and salt; it must be dry, but not burnt. It is excellent when stewed with pork chops."

Mary Randolph, *The Virginia Housewife or, Methodical Cook; a facsimile of an authentic early American cookbook*

BAKED ACORN AND BUTTERED SQUASH

After washing squash, cut it in half and remove seeds. Rub oil or butter inside squash, and add salt and pepper to taste. Bake at 375° for about 30–45 minutes.

Honey, maple syrup, or brown sugar can be added to squash before baking, or before serving.

From *Backcountry Housewife*, Schiele Museum. 1985.

Turnips

Turnips were a staple food on the frontier. They were easy to grow and long-lasting. Turnips were often used as we would use potatoes today in soups and stews.

"Peel off half an inch of the stringy outside. Full grown turnips will take about an hour and a half of gentle boiling; if you slice them, which most people do, they will be done sooner; try them with a fork, and when tender, take them up, and lay them on a sieve till the water is thoroughly drained from them; send them up whole."

Cooking with Mary Alexander, Hezekiah Alexander Homesite. Charlotte, NC.

Note: *Send them up* means take them to the table to serve.

TO MASH TURNIPS
"When they are boiled quite tender, squeeze them as dry as possible, put them into a sauce pan, mash them with a wooden spoon and rub them through a colander; add a little bit of butter, keep stirring them till the butter is melted and well mixed with them, and they are ready for table."

Cooking with Mary Alexander, Hezekiah Alexander Homesite. Charlotte, NC.

Carrots

"The yellow are better than the orange or red; middling sized, that is, a foot long and two inches thick at the top end, are better than over grown ones."
—Amelia Simmons, *The First American Cookbook*

CARROT PUDDING

"A cupful of boiled and strained carrots, 5 eggs, 2 ounces of sugar and butter each, cinnamon and rose-water to your taste, baked in a deep dish without paste."

Amelia Simmons, *The First American Cookbook, A Facsimile of "American Cookery,"* 1796.

A CARROT PUDDING

"Boil some good carrots; and when they are well clean'd, weight half a pound of them, beat them very fine in a mortar; mix 2 or 3 spoonfuls of sweet cream along with them; beat eight eggs, keeping out half of the whites, with half a pound of sugar; mix all well together, and season it with beat cinnamon, or orange grate, if you have it, so it makes it eat like an orange pudding. Mix 6 ounces of cast butter in just when you are about putting it into the oven. For Sauce, take an half mutchkin of cream, sweeten with a little sugar, and add to it the squeeze of a lemon."

Mrs. Frazer, *The Practice of Cookery, Pastry, Pickling, Preserving, &c.*, 1791.

Cabbage

FRIED CABBAGE - *Adaptation*

Cabbage was a common vegetable in the kitchen gardens of early settlers. It was easy to preserve and could last through part of the winter months. Cabbage could be eaten raw, cooked, or fermented as kraut.

shredded or chopped cabbage
bacon drippings or vegetable oil

Fry 2 or 3 slices of bacon, or use leftover bacon grease. Heat grease in a cast iron skillet. Toss in cabbage and stir. When thoroughly heated, turn heat to low, and cook until cabbage is tender. A small amount of water can be added if needed. Do not add salt since the salty flavor will come from the bacon drippings. Crumble bacon pieces into cabbage and add other seasonings if you like, such as lemon pepper.

Note: although using bacon grease is a more authentic frontier style of cooking, for this recipe you may substitute vegetable oil or olive oil if you prefer. If so, add a little salt to taste.

Tullie's Receipts. Atlanta Historical Society.

COLE SLAW

"Wash & clean a fresh cabbage, shave down the head in very thin strips, with a sharp knife, and put it into the salad dish, then prepare the following dressing. Stir gradually into a table spoonful of mustard flour, one large table spoonful of the best olive oil; when the mustard had absorbed all the oil, add a spoonful of salt, a little cayenne, and the yolk of two eggs boiled hard, mix these until they are of the consistence of soft butter; then stir into the mixture a tea cupful of cold vinegar, & pour this dressing over the cabbage just as it goes to the table, the cabbage will lose its freshness by standing a long time in the dressing."

Handwritten script in a notebook, Florida State Archives.

COLE SLAW — *For Today's Cook*

The name comes from the Dutch wood "koolsalade," meaning "cabbage salad." Coleslaw can be made in a variety of ways. Here is one example.

4 c. thinly sliced red or green cabbage
1/3 c. red wine vinegar
¼ c. vegetable oil or melted butter
salt and freshly ground pepper to taste

Mix all ingredients and set aside before serving to give the flavors time to blend well.

TO MAKE SOUR KROUT [Sauerkraut]

"Take your fine hard white cabbage, cut them very small, have a tub on purpose with the head out, according to the quantity you intend to make; put them in the tub, to every four or five cabbages throw in a large handful of salt; when you have done as many as you intend, lay a very heavy weight on them to press them down as flat as possible, throw a cloth over them and lay on the cover; let them stand a month, then you may begin to use it. It will keep twelve months, but be sure to keep it always close-covered, and the weight on it; if you throw a few caraway seeds pounded fine amongst it, they give it a fine flavour. The way to dress it is with a fine fat piece of beef stewed together. It is a dish made much use of amongst the Germans, and in the North Countries, where the frost kills all the cabbages; therefore they preserve them in this manner before the frost takes them. Cabbage stalks, cauliflower stalks, and artichokes-stalks peel, and cut fine down in the same manner, are very good."

Hannah Glasse, *The Art of Cookery Made Plain and Easy*, 1747.

Parsnips

"Parsnips are a valuable root cultivated best in rich old grounds and doubly deep plowed "

—Amelia Simmons, *The First American Cookbook*

TO MASH PARSNIPS

"Boil them tender, scape [scrape] them clean, then scape all the soft into a Sauce-pan, put as much Milk or Cream, as will stew them. Keep them stirring, and when quite thick, stir in a good Piece of Butter, and send them to the Table."

Hannah Glasse, *The Art of Cookery Made Plain and Easy,* 1747

TO DRESS PARSNIPS TO EAT LIKE SKIRRETS

"Boil some large parsnips tender, and scrape off the skins; cut them by the length, and cut every piece round, about the size of a skirret, and fry them in butter a fine light brown; take them out of the butter, and lay them neatly in a dish. Strew beat cinnamon and sugar over them before you send them to the table."

Mrs. Frazer, *The Practice of Cookery, 1791.*

Note: *Skirrets* are an almost forgotten Tudor root crop similar to carrots and parsnips. The white skinny roots are sweet and most pleasant. In Scotland they are known as Cummocks.

Corn

CORN ROASTED IN THE HUSKS

This common way to prepare corn on the frontier was learned from Native American cooking traditions.

Carefully pull back husks from freshly picked corn and gently remove silks. Replace husks around the cob, and tie with a strip of husk or cord. Soak the corn in water for 1 hour.

Place corn on the grill over hot, glowing coals, or place in hot ashes at the fireplace. Corn can be cooked on a grill over a campfire, as well. Do not place corn directly on fire.

Turn corn often until the husks are steaming about 15–20 minutes. Then remove husks, and serve with butter and seasonings. Cooking time may vary depending on how hot the coals are and the distance of the grill top to the hot coals.

CORN PUDDING – *Miss Everitt*

"12 ears of corn grated, a quart of sweet milk, a quarter of a lb of fresh butter, 2 eggs well beaten. Pepper & salt to the taste. Stire all together, bake in a buttered dish for three hours."

Handwritten script in a notebook, Florida Archives.

CORN PUDDING

"Grate the corn, add to a quart of it, a tea cup full of cream or milk, a lump of butter about the size of an egg, a spoon full of salt, mix it all well together, put it in the dish and bake an hour & a half."

Handwritten script in a notebook, Florida Archives.

TO MAKE AN OATMEAL HASTY PUDDING

"Take a Quart of Water, set it on to boil, put in a Piece of Butter, some Salt, when it boils, stir in the Oatmeal as you do the flour till it is of a good Thickness; let it boil a few minutes, pour it in your Dish, and stick Pieces of Butter in it; or eat with Wine and Sugar, or Cream or new Milk. This is best made with Scotch oatmeal."

Hannah Glasse, *The Art of Cookery Made Plain and Easy*, 1747.

BUTTERED WHEAT

"Put your Wheat into a Sauce-pan, when it is hot, stir in a good Piece of Butter, a little grated Nutmeg, and sweeten to your Palate."

Hannah Glasse, *The Art of Cookery Made Plain and Easy*, 1747.

BARLEY SOUP

Barley is a grain sometimes overlooked when rice, corn, and wheat are predominant. This soup is almost a stew. Though simple in preparation, the meat and vegetables make it a dish that is filling and satisfying.

"Put on three gills of barley, three quarts of water, a few onions cut up, six carrots, scraped and cut into dice, an equal quantity of turnips cut small; boil it gently two hours, then put in four or five pounds of the rack or neck of mutton, a few slices of lean ham, with pepper and salt; boil it slowly, two hours longer, and serve it up."

Mary Randolph, *The Virginia Housewife*

Note: A *gill* is equal to 1/4 pint.

BARLEY SOUP - *For Today's Cook*

¾ c. barley, rinsed
1½ quarts water
2 medium onions, peeled and diced
3 medium carrots, scraped and diced
3 medium turnips, peeled and diced
1½ pounds lamb, diced (or beef if desired)
½ c. ham, diced
salt and pepper to taste

Put water into large saucepan or Dutch-oven and add barley and diced meat. Bring to a boil and reduce heat and simmer for 45 minutes. Add diced onions, carrots, and turnips and simmer for 20 minutes until carrots are tender. Add diced ham. Simmer for 20 minutes up to one hour. Season to taste with salt and pepper.

HAM TOAST

"Take a quarter pound of lean Ham [boiled] chop in small [pieces], the yoke of 3 eggs well beaten, ½ ounce of butter, 2 table-spoons of cream and a little cayenne (or black pepper) and stir it over the fire till it thickens, and spread it on hot toast. Garish with parsley."

From General William Lenoir Papers, Fort Defiance, Lenoir, NC.

EGG AND BACON PIE TO EAT COLD

"Steep a few thin slices of bacon all night in water to take out the salt, lay your bacon in the dish, beat eight eggs with a pint of thick cream, put in a little pepper and salt, and pour it on the bacon, lay over it a good cold paste, bake it a day before you want it in a moderate oven."

Hannah Glasse, *The Art of Cookery Made Plain and Easy*, 1774

DESSERTS

Puddings

Puddings were very common in the 18th century and could be baked or boiled in a cloth or bag. Hannah Glasse, in her 1755 cookbook edition, writes:

> "In boiled Puddings, take great Care the Bag or Cloth be very clean, not soapy, but dipped in hot Water and well floured. If a Bread pudding, tie is loose; if a Batter-pudding, tie it close; and be sure the Water boils when you put the Pudding in, and you should move the Puddings in the Pot now and then, for fear they stick...."

I used the following Hannah Glasse receipt at Latta Plantation. It was always a success and enjoyed by volunteers and friends.

AN ORDINARY BREAD PUDDING

"Take two Halfpenny Roles, slice them thin, Crust and all, pour over them a Pint of new Milk boiling hot, cover them close, let it stand some Hours to soak; then beat it well with a little melted Butter, and beat the Yolks and Whites of two Eggs, beat all together well with a little Salt. Boil it an half Hour; when it is done, turn it into your Dish, pour melted Butter over it and Sugar, some love a little Vinegar in the Butter. If your Roles are stale and grated, they will do better; add a little Ginger. You make bake it with a few Currants."   Hannah Glasse, *The Art of Cookery Made Plain and Easy*, 1747.

Note: *Halfpenny roles* were a common bread in the 18th century and were half the size of a penny loaf.

For this recipe use an unsliced loaf of bread. Use enough bread to make a good pudding with the amounts of ingredients called for. You can also bake the pudding in a buttered dish in a Dutch-oven.

HOW TO MAKE BAG PUDDINGS

Bag puddings were made in a tightly woven cloth bag made of linen or a piece of linen material gathered at the top and tied with a string. The bag or cloth must be wet and rubbed with butter and dredged with flour. This process is similar to greasing a baking pan to keep from sticking. If you are using a bag, it is the inside lining that is to be buttered. (The bag is similar to a flour sack.) Place the bag or cloth in a large bowl buttered and floured side up. Arrange the bag or cloth to the edges of the bowl before pouring in the pudding mixture. Tie the top of the bag or the edges of the cloth securely. Put it into a pot of boiling water where it has plenty of room. Keep another pot of hot water close at hand so more water can be added if needed to keep the water level high. Cover the pot. When done, dip the pudding in cold water so you can unwrap it. Cooking times will vary. If you open the bag or cloth and see that the pudding is not firm enough to keep its form then tie it up again and boil it more. This pudding is good served warm and also slightly fried in butter for breakfast.

Elizabeth McAnulty, Camp Cookery, Recipes for Revolutionary War Re-enactors, 1989.

Note: It is important to prevent the bag from sticking to the bottom of the pot. There are several ways this can be done. If the pot is large enough, place a thin flat rock, plate, or shallow wooden bowl in the bottom of the pot. Another way is to attach the bag to a sturdy stick that can sit across the top of the pot. This allows the bag to be suspended in the water without touching the bottom of the pot.

A PLAIN RICE PUDDING

"Pick and wash a pint of rice, and boil it soft. Then drain off the water, and let the rice dry and get cold. Afterwards mix with it two ounces of butter, and 4 ounces sugar, and stir it into a quart of rich milk. Beat 4 or 5 eggs very light, and add them gradually to the mixture. Stir in at the last a table-spoonfull of mixed nutmeg and cinnamon. Bake it an hour in a deep dish. Eat it cold."

L. L. Senseman, *Receipts*, 1844-1854.

A NICE INDIAN PUDDING

"3 pints scalded milk, 7 spoons of fine Indian meal, stir together while hot. Let stand till cooled; add 7 eggs, half pound of raisins, 4 ounces butter, spice, and sugar; bake one and a half hour."

Amelia Simmons, *The First American Cookbook,*1796.

Portions for Today's Cook:
1 pint cream (2 c.) + 10 oz. of cornmeal (1 ¼ c.) + 3 oz. of raisins (6 Tbsp.) + 3 oz. of sugar (6 Tbsp.) + 1½ tsp. ground cinnamon, nutmeg and cloves + 1½ oz. of melted butter (3 Tablespoons) + 3 eggs

INDIAN PUDDING - *For Today's Cook*

1 ¼ c. plain cornmeal

2 c. hot milk

¼ c. sugar

1/8 tsp. baking soda

½ tsp. salt

½ tsp. ginger

½ tsp. cinnamon

¼ c. molasses

1 c. cold milk

whipped cream

nutmeg

Heat milk in a heavy pan and stir in cornmeal, a little at a time. Cook for 15 minutes or until mixture becomes thick, stirring constantly. Remove from heat. Mix together sugar, baking soda, salt, ginger, and cinnamon. Add this to the cornmeal mixture, along with the molasses and cold milk, stirring until all ingredients are mixed together thoroughly. Pour into a baking dish and bake at 275° for about 2 hours. Serve warm with whipped cream and a light sprinkling of freshly-grated nutmeg.

Cakes

JANE KNOX LATTA'S GINGERCAKE

This is an adaptation of an 19th century receipt from Latta Plantation in Huntersville, North Carolina. I have cooked at the hearth there many times. In colonial days, ginger cakes were prepared for special occasions such as Christmas. They are especially tasty topped with whipped cream or lemon sauce.

Rebecca may have baked gingercake for her children at Christmas.

2 c. molasses
1 c. sugar
1 c. lard
1 c. milk
1 tsp. soda
2 tsp. ginger
4 eggs
2 pints flour, or enough to make batter stiff (approx. 4 cups)

Beat sugar and shortening thoroughly. Add eggs and molasses. Sift soda, ginger, and flour together. Add flour mixture and milk. Pour this mixture into a well-greased pan, and bake at 350° about 30 minutes, or until a knife inserted in the center comes out clean.

YORK GINGERBREAD

"6 teacups sugar, 3 butter, 3 molasses, 3 milk, 9 flour, 1 ginger, 6 eggs, 2 teaspoons pearlash dissolved in two tablespoons vinegar, 1 cup orange peel & spice. Bake in a loafe."

Domestic Skills Program, Old Salem, 1988.

Note: *Pearlash* was an early version of baking soda.

From the manuscript receipt collection of Louisa Senseman (1822-1854), the daughter of Salem silversmith John Vogler. The adaptation below uses modern measurements but keeps the same proportions:

YORK GINGERBREAD — *For Today's Cook*

Cream 1 c. + 2 Tbsp. soft butter and 2¼ c. sugar. Add 3 medium eggs, beating after each addition. Add and mix in 1 c. + 2 Tbsp. molasses, 1/4 c. + 2 Tbsp. peeled, sliced, and chopped ginger root, 1/3 c. grated orange peel (2-3 oranges), 1 tsp. cinnamon, 1/8 tsp. ground cloves. In a separate cup combine 1 Tbsp. vinegar, 1 tsp. baking soda. Mix in. Add alternately 1 c. + 2 Tbsp. milk and 3¼ c. all-purpose flour, mixing after each addition. Pour into a greased and floured 9x13 pan. Bake at 375° for 50-55 minutes or until done in the middle.

TO MAKE ORING [Orange] CAKES

"Take ye pill of 4 Oringes being first pared ye meat taken out, boyle them tender beat them small in a Morter of marble, then tak ye meat o them & 2 more Oringes, the seeds and skin being picked out, & mix it wih ye pill that are beat sett it on ye fire with a Spoonfull of Oring flower watter, keep it stiring till the Mixster be pretty well dryed up; then have ready to every pound of pulp a pound and a quarter of Double refined sugar, make ye Suger very hott and dry upon ye fire then mix it with ye pulp & sett it over ye fire again till ye Sugar be melted but be sure it do not boyle; then you may put a little of the pills fine cutt or greated, and when it is cold drop it upon double paper and dry it before ye fire when you turn them put 2 together or you may keep them in deep glasses or potts."

Tryon Palace Commission, *A Tryon Palace Trifle or Eighteenth Century Cookery, Etc.*, (New Bern, NC: Tryon Palace, 1960).

BLACK CAKE

"2 cups molasses, 1 cup of sugar, 1 [cup] of butter, 1 cup of sour cream, 5 eggs, 6 cups of flour, 2 spoonful[s] of ginger, 1 teaspoonful of soda. Bake an hour."

From General William Lenoir Papers, Fort Defiance, Lenoir, NC.

This receipt is not dated but because soda is an ingredient, it is probably from the 19th century. The cake turns out best when using fresh, unsulfured molasses, real butter, plain unbleached flour and fresh ginger.

A FINE PLUMB-CAKE

Eighteenth century Christmas in the Carolina backcountry was quite different than the festivities we experience today. In colonial times Christmas was more a religious holiday and some-times 12th Night was the more exciting time. It was a time for gathering of family and neighbors mingled with merriment, good food and cheer. Decorations, if any, were simple. Evergreens, holly berries, and herbs may have been placed on the mantel, table or around the doorway. Christmas trees were unheard of except per-haps in the Moravian communities. Sometimes special dishes or sweets were prepared that required expensive spices, dried fruits, or sugar. Music would not be the sounds of carols as we know them today but rather traditional tunes or jigs from the old country. This is probably the kind of Christmas celebration Rebecca Boone and her family shared.

One of the dishes I have prepared at the Cleveland hearth in Wilkesboro is "A fine Plumb-cake." The receipt is from Mrs. Frazer's 1791 cookbook printed in Edinburgh.

"Take one pound and half of eggs, and whisk them till they be very thick and light. Beat and searce one half pound of sugar; mix into your eggs by degrees, and keep casting till it be very light. Stone and mince half a pound raisins; clean half a pound currants; blanch and cut half a pound of almonds; cut half a pound of orange-peel, and half a pound of citron small; cast three quarters of a pound of sweet butter to a cream; mix all these together, and season with quarter of a pound of cinnamon; a grated nutmeg, and half an ounce of powdered ginger. Butter your hoop and put your mixture into it. Smooth the top with a knife, and strew four ounces of carraways over it. Put in a quick oven."

"Plumb" is another word for plum but in the 18th century it also meant dried fruits such as raisins, currants, cherries or figs. All measurements are given in weights, not by cups, numbers or teaspoons. "Searce" means to sift.

A RICH SEED CAKE

"Take four pounds of the finest flour, and three pounds of double-refined sugar beaten and sifted; mix them together, and dry them by the fire till you prepare the other materials; take four pounds of butter, beat it with your hand till it is soft like cream; then beat thirty-five eggs, leave out sixteen whites, strain off your eggs from the threads, and beat them and the butter together till all appears like butter. Put in four or five spoonfuls of rose or orange-flower water, and beat again; then take your flour and sugar, with six ounces of carraway-seeds, and strew them in by degrees, beating it all the time for two hours together; you may put in as much tincture of cinnamon or amber grease as you please, butter your hoop, and let it stand three hours in a moderate oven. You must observe always, in beating of butter, to do it with a cool hand, and beat it always one way in a deep earthen dish."

Hannah Glasse, *The Art of Cookery Made Plain and Easy*, 1747.

For Today's Cook:

2 c. good quality butter
6 c. plain unbleached flour
6 whole eggs, and another 5 egg yolks
3 Tbsp. orange or rose flower water
3 c. sugar
1/3 c. caraway seeds
1/2 tsp. cinnamon

Pies & Fruit Desserts

APPLE PIE - *For Today's Cook*

Prepare your favorite crust ahead of time and use it for this delicious pie. You will need both a top and a bottom crust. Use a large pie dish.

8 large apples, sliced thin
½ c. sugar or sweeten to taste
½ tsp. grated nutmeg
1 tsp. cinnamon
1 Tbsp. butter

Use fresh, tart cooking apples or dried apples that have been soaked and cooked until tender. Wash apples well. Peel or keep natural.

Line pie pan with crust and then fill with apples. Mix together spices, sugar, and sprinkle over apples. Add bits of butter and then place top crust over fruit. Crimp or press the edges of the top and bottom crust together. Prick top 3–4 times with fork. Bake at 375° for about 1 hour.

Note: Sweeten pie to taste with sugar or honey and use spices of choice. Whisked up egg white brushed on top crust will give it a shiny gloss. A colonial cook like Rebecca Boone would use whatever was available to make her pies. This pie made with honey is wonderful. Use about 1/2 cup honey and drizzle over apples and spices before adding top crust.

Apple Pie based on *Recipes from the Raleigh Tavern Bake Shop*, The Colonial Williamsburg Foundation: Williamsburg, VA.

PUFF PASTE

"Take a quarter of a peck of flour, run in a pound of butter very fine, make it up in a light paste with cold water, just stiff enough to work it up; then roll it up about as thick as a crown-piece, put a layer of butter all over; sprinkle on a little flour, double it up, and roll it out again; double it, and roll it three times; then it is fit for all sorts of pies and tarts that require a puff-paste."

Hannah Glasse, *The Art of Cookery Made Plain and Easy*, 1747.

Note: a *crown-piece* is an old British coin.

CINNAMON PIE - *Traditional*

Prepare 1 pie crust, and have it ready. Preheat the oven so that it is nice and hot. This works well in a Dutch-oven.

2 eggs, slightly beaten
½ c. sugar
3 Tbsp. flour
1½ c. milk or light cream
2 tsp. cinnamon

Beat together all ingredients in a bowl. Pour mixture into an unbaked pie crust and bake at 325° for about 25–30 minutes or until a knife inserted in the center comes out clean.

BLACK CAPS

"Cut your Apples in half. Lay them on a Mazarine Dish or for want of that on the Brim of another Dish. Your Apples must not be Pared lay the cut side upon the Dish, wet the top of your Apples about an Inch square with White Wine, and strew Fine Sugar upon the Wett Place and bake them. Take care they don't Fall too much in the Oven."

Richard J. Hooker, ed., *A Colonial Plantation Cookbook: The Receipt Book of Harriott Pinckney Horry*, 1770 (Columbia, SC: University of South Carolina Press, 1984).

Notes: Mazarine (French) or Mazarin today, refers to a deep pie dish or pan made of fine metal or porcelain. When prepared at the Cleveland House a large redware pottery pie dish was used that worked perfectly.

During baking, the skins of the apples may turn darker, depending on the type of apples used, resulting in black tops or caps.

WILD FRUIT COBBLER - *Traditional*

Any kind of fresh fruit can be adapted to this recipe. On the frontier Rebecca Boone could find many kinds of wild fruit—strawberries, blueberries, plums, blackberries, or cherries. In addition, she may have picked fruit from local orchards.

Portions of ingredients would often depend on the amount of fruit picked, and what was stored in the kitchen cupboard. If sugar was not available, honey or maple syrup would have been used to sweeten this dessert.

Recipe and directions continue on next page.

Crust mixture:

> 1 qt. flour
> 4 Tbsp. melted butter or lard
> ½ tsp. salt
> 2 tsp. baking powder (optional)
> milk or water

Cobbler mixture:

> 3 Tbsp. flour
> 3 Tbsp. sugar
> about 6 c. fresh fruit
> 1 teacup full of sugar

Mix all dry ingredients together, then add enough milk or water to form a soft dough. Separate the dough into 2 balls—one for lining the bottom of the baking dish and one for covering the top of the fruit.

Roll both balls of the dough out thin. Use one to line the baking dish and form the bottom crust. Mix 3 Tbsp. flour and 3 Tbsp. sugar together and sprinkle over bottom crust. Pour in the fresh fruit, enough to fill the baking dish. Cover fruit with 1 teacup of sugar. Place top crust over fruit and crimp or press the edges of the top and bottom crust together. Make 2 or 3 slits in the top crust with a small knife. Bake in a quick oven for about 30 minutes.

Note: a teacup used for measuring ingredients holds less than a standard 8 oz. cup; a teacup holds about 6 oz.

ANOTHER WAY TO MAKE A BERRY COBBLER - *Traditional*

Mix 2 cups of berries with ¾ c. sugar, or sweeten to your taste. Cook berries and sugar over medium heat, stirring and mashing the berries to make a thick mixture. Put sweetened berry mixture

into a buttered baking dish. Cover with strips of rolled-out pastry dough and top with bits of butter. Bake at 450° until golden brown and the fruit mixture is bubbling.

TO MAKE A CHERRY, PLUMB, OR GOOSEBERRY PIE

"Make a good crust, lay a little round the sides of your dish, throw sugar at the bottom, and lay in your fruit and sugar at top. A few red currants does well with them; put on your lid, and bake it in a slack oven.

Make a plumb pie the same way, and a gooseberry pie. If you would have it red, let it stand a good while in the oven after the bread is drawn. A custard is very good with a gooseberry pie."

Susannah Carter, *The Frugal Housewife or, Complete Woman Cook; The American Antiquarian Cookbook Collection*

Note: This receipt also works well with peaches and apples.

Cookies

Note: In the 18th century, *cakes* meant cookies.

ABIGAIL'S SOFT MOLASSES CAKES – *For Today's Cook*

These little cakes are a favorite with Crane House visitors of all ages. They should be soft and large. Serve hot with cool milk.

2½ c. sifted flour	½ c. sugar
2 tsp. baking soda	½ c. molasses
1 tsp. ginger	1 egg
1 tsp. cinnamon	¼ c. cold water
¼ tsp. salt	1 c. light raisins
½ c. soft butter	

Sift flour, baking soda, ginger, cinnamon, and salt together. Beat butter, sugar, molasses, and egg together until light and fluffy. Add sifted ingredients alternately with cold water. Mix until blended. Stir in raisins. Drop by rounded tablespoonfuls 3 inches apart on greased baking sheet. Bake 10 to 12 minutes at 350°. Size should be approximately 4 inches across.

Fanny Pierson Crane, *Fanny Pierson Crane: Her Receipts, 1796.*

TO MAKE GINGERBREAD CAKES

"Take three pounds of flour, one pound of sugar, one pound of butter rubbed in very fine, two ounces of ginger beat fine, a large nutmeg grated; then take a pound of treacle, a quart of a pint of cream, make them warm together, and make up the bread stiff; roll it out, and make it up into thin cakes, cut them out with a tea-cup, or small glass, or roll them round like nuts, and bake them on tin plates in a slack oven."

Hannah Glasse, *The Art of Cookery Made Plain and Easy, 1747 & 1796.*

Note: *Treacle* is a British term for molasses. *Slack* describes a moderately warm oven.

ANOTHER SORT OF LITTLE CAKES

"A pound of flour, and half a pound of sugar; beat half a pound of butter with your hand, and mix them well together; bake it in little cakes." Hannah Glasse, *The Art of Cookery Made Plain and Easy*, 1747.

TO MAKE THE BEST SHORT BREAD

"Take a peck of flour, and keep out about a pound of it; beat and searce a pound of loaf sugar, and cut a pound of orange peel, half a pound of citron, and one half pound of blanched almonds; mix them all well together with your flour and make a hole in the middle of it; rind three pounds of sweet butter with a tsp. of salt, and half a mutchkin of good barm; work it, but not too much; divide the paste into four quarters, and make up each quarter into an oval; then roll out each quarter by itself into what thickness you please with the flour you kept out, and cut it through the middle, so as to have two fardels out of each quarter; prickle it well on the top, pinch it round with your fingers, and strew caraways on the top. If you want it plain, keep out the sugar and fruits and in place of three pounds of butter, take two pounds, and mix with half a mutchkin of water and half a mutchkin of more barm. Fire in slow oven."

Mrs. Frazier, *The Practice of Cookery, Pastry, Pickling, Preserving, &c.*, 1791.

Note: A *peck* is equal to 2 dry gallons, 8 dry quarts, or 16 dry pints. To *searce* is to sift. A *mutchkin* is 1/4 pint. A *barm* is the foam, or scum, formed on the top. A *fardel* is 1/4 of a circle.

SHORTBREAD – *For Today's Cook*

For this recipe, follow the directions exactly.

½ c. white sugar
1 c. butter, softened
2 c. plain flour

Mix all ingredients together by hand until they are well blended. Form into balls about the size of a quarter. Place balls on a baking sheet, and press each in center with finger. Bake at 275° for about 30 minutes. If your oven cooks fast, adjust the temperature to a lower setting. Shortbread should not get brown. Let shortbread cool on pan, and then remove.

James K. Polk Memorial, Charlotte, NC.

SHROWSBURY CAKES

"Mix a pound of searced sugar, and a pound of flowre well together. Then beat & searce some sinamon, nutmegg, & ginger, & put in 2 egg youlks. Worke all these to paste with sweet butter, and roule it about halfe an inch thick. Cut them round, & flowre your papers, & soe bake them & when they looke ised [iced] over, they are enough."

Martha Washington, *Martha Washington's Booke of Cookery and Booke of Sweetmeats*

Note: The receipt above is written in old English. Shrewsbury Cakes are named for Shrewsbury, England, located near the Welsh border. There are many variations of this popular British receipt. This one is a favorite.

SHROWSBURY CAKES - *For Today's Cook:*

2 c. sugar
3 c. plain flour
½ tsp. each of cinnamon, nutmeg, and ginger
2 egg yolks
2 c. butter

Mix sugar and flour. Add spices. Add beaten yolks. Then work into paste with butter. Roll out ½ inch thick and cut in rounds. Bake at 400°. Finely chopped walnuts or hickory nuts may be added. Cooking with Mary Alexander, Hezekiah Alexander Homesite, 1985.

FRUIT CREAMS

Fruit and heavy cream mixed together make a good breakfast in the summer. This was very popular in the 18th century. Use fresh fruit of choice or a combination.

Elizabeth McAnulty, Camp Cookery, Recipes for Revolutionary War Re-enactors, 1989.

THOMAS JEFFERSON'S ICED CREAM - *For Today's Cook*

The first time I made this delectable dessert was at the back-country cabins at Iredell Museum where I was Director. Since then it has been a pleasure to provide this demonstration for visitors and re-enactors alike at several events. It even won first prize in a local ice cream contest made the old-fashioned way.

Creating this hand-made treat with the sorbetiere in a bucket of ice is a wonderful attraction and is a way to engage visitors by allowing them to help turn the cream. When we break open the sorbetiere for tasting we always get the same acclamation, "this is the best ice cream I have ever had!"

In the late 18th century, local rivers and ponds froze over. Some of the area plantations and large farms had ice houses. Large chunks of ice were cut out of the Catawba and Yadkin Rivers and stored in straw, hay, or sawdust which provided insulation, keeping the ice from melting. The ice was not used to put in drinks but to cool them down or keep items cold or perhaps to make ice cream.

Thomas Jefferson and George Washington both enjoyed iced cream and Dollie Madison served it at the White House during her husband's Presidency. I have made Thomas Jefferson's receipt rolled in a barrel of ice and for a sorbet in a bucket of ice. Both turned out wonderfully causing many taste testers to say it was the best they had ever tasted.

Jefferson's receipt can also be made in a modern ice cream maker and can be served plain or with fruit, cookies, or cake.

Recipe and directions continue on next page.

one quart rich cream

6 egg yolks

1 cup sugar

Combine egg yolks and sugar. Mix well and set aside.

Place one quart cream and whole vanilla bean into heavy sauce pan and bring to almost a boil. Stir occasionally.

Gently pour into egg mixture and stir well. Return to heat and bring to boiling stage but do not boil. Stir as needed to keep from sticking.

Remove from heat and strain. Let cool for a few minutes before pouring into sorbetiere or ice cream maker.

Surround maker with three parts ice to one part salt. Begin cranking.

Note: A sorbetiere is a french ice cream maker. It is a cylindrical container that has a lid with a handle. In colonial times the sorbetiere was placed in a bucket of ice and salt and twisted or turned in a back and forth motion until the cream was set. Occasionally the container would be checked to see if it was ready or to scoop the side of frozen cream to the middle of the container.

When ready, the iced cream was allowed to set for about 10 minutes then served. Sometimes it was placed in a mould and kept frozen until solid and then served immediately. This was a very unusual and impressive dessert for guests.

For best results use the best cream and eggs available, and the whole vanilla bean.

Marie Kimball, *Thomas Jefferson's Cookbook*, University of Virginia Press, 1976.

BEVERAGES

HOW TO MAKE TEA PROPERLY

"The proper way to make a good cup of tea is a matter of some importance. The plan which I have practiced for these twelve months is this. The teapot is at once filled up with boiling water, then the tea is put into the pot, and is allowed to stand for five minutes before it is used; the leaves gradually absorb the water, and as gradually sink to the bottom; the result is that the tea leaves are not scalded as they are when boiling water is poured over them, and you get to the true flavor of the tea. In truth much less tea is required in this way than under the old common practice."

James Cuthill. William Lenoir Papers. London.

BLACKBERRY SHRUB

"The best thirst quenchers were fruit shrubs—sweet to the taste but tart and tingley on the back of the throat. 2 lbs of fresh blackberries. 4 cups good cider vinegar 4 cups sugar. Let blackberries soak for three days in vinegar in covered glass container at room temperature. Then pour vinegar and blackberries into a fine mesh strainer pressing down to extract as much juice as possible. Pour liquid into saucepan, add the sugar, bring to a boil stirring constantly until sugar has dissolved. Boil mixture for about two minutes remove from heat and cool. To serve: add 1/4 cup blackberry syrup to one cup cold water in a tall glass."

James K. Polk Memorial, Charlotte, NC.

A COOLING CINNAMON WATER IN HOT WEATHER

Boil one gallon of water, pour it into a gallon demijohn, set this before the fire, then put into it twelve cloves, two ounces of whole cinnamon, then stop up your bottle and put in in a cool place; When you want to mix your liquor, put half a pint into two quarts of water, with one quarter pound of sugar, cool it in ice before you serve it, and it is a most wholesome and delicious drink as you can take in hot weather.

Robert Roberts, *The House Servant's Directory*, Boston, 1827.

Note: In the 18th century this was an alcoholic drink, but in the early 19th century we find that it was being used with just water and sweetened to taste. It is a very refreshing drink with honey as the sweetener. Ice was not added to the drink but was used to cool the drink by placing a pitcher in a container of crushed ice. Cool spring or well water works fine.

MINT TEA - *Traditional*

Pour boiling or very hot water over fresh mint leaves. Allow to stand about five minutes. Remove mint leaves and sweeten to taste. Serve either hot or cold.

SASSAFRAS TEA - *Traditional*

Dry the bark of the root of the sassafras tree. Pour boiling or very hot water over the dried root. Allow to rest until water is flavored. Remove the sassafras, sweeten to taste. Serve hot or cold.

GLOSSARY OF TERMS

baking dish—casserole dish

barm—the foam, or scum, formed on the top

demijohn—a big jug or bottle with a narrow neck for beverage storage

fardel—1/4 of a circle.

foraging—gathering wild greens, nuts or berries

gill—A gill is equal to 1/4 pint and is pronounced "jill."

sorbetiere—ice cream maker

iron—cast iron

mutchkin—equals 1/4 pint

pearlash—refined potassium car-bonate, an alkaline salt found in wood ashes that also goes by the name potash. It was once used to leaven things like corn cakes. If you are using an old recipe that calls for pearlash, just substitute baking soda but use about half again as much.

peck—equal to 2 dry gallons, 8 dry quarts, or 16 dry pints

penny loaf bread—see p. 94.

plumb—another word for plum but in the 18th century it also meant dried fruits such as raisins, currants, cherries, figs, etc.

puncheon—A piece of broad, heavy, roughly dressed timber with one face finished flat

quick oven—a hot oven, about 375-400° Fahrenheit.

receipt—recipe. The word *receipt* is a very old term that can be traced back to the Medieval Latin word meaning to take or receive. It was commonly used in cook-books until just after the Civil War. Today the word *recipe* has replaced the old term.

searce—sift

skirrets—an almost forgotten Tudor root crop similar to carrots and parsnips. The white skinny roots are sweet and most pleas-ant. In Scotland they are know as Cummocks.

soda—baking soda

BIBLIOGRAPHY

Andrews, Mrs. Lewis R. and Mrs. J. Reany Kelly, editors. *The Hammond-Harwood House cookbook.* Annapolis, Maryland: The Hammond-Harwood House Association, 1964.

Atlanta Historical Society. *Tullie's Receipts: Nineteenth Century Plantation Plain Style Southern Cooking and Living.* Atlanta, Georgia: The Conger Printing and Publishing Co. 1976

Betts, Edwin Morris, ed. *Thomas Jefferson's Garden Book, 1766-1824: With Relevant Extracts from His Other Writings.* Charlottesville, Virginia: Thomas Jefferson Foundation, Inc. 2012.

Brawley, James S. *Rowan County...a brief history.* Raleigh, North Carolina: North Carolina Department of Cultural Resources, Division of Archives and History, Revised, 1977.

Bullock, Helen. *The Williamsburg Art of Cookery.* Williamsburg, Virginia: Colonial Williamsburg Foundation. 1992.

Carter, Susannah. *The Frugal Housewife or, Complete Woman Cook; The American Antiquarian Cookbook Collection.* Kansas City, Missouri: Andrews McMeel Publishing, LLC, 2013.

Cooking in the Latta Kitchen. Latta Plantation, North Carolina, 1992.

Cooking with Mary Alexander. Hezekiah Alexander Homeside. 1985.

Cultivated Plants of the Wachovia Tract in North Carolina, 1759-1764. Compiled by Flora Ann L. Bynum. Winston Salem, North Carolina: Old Salem, Inc. 1979.

Culpeper, Nicholas. David Potterton, editor. *Culpeper's Color Herbal.* New York, New York: Sterling Publishing Co., Inc. 1983.

Farmers, Dennis & Carol. *The King's Bread, 2d Rising: Cooking at Niagara, 1726-1815.* Youngston, New York: Old Fort Niagara Association, Inc. 1989.

Fettiplace, Elinor. Hilary Spurling, editor. *Elinor Fettiplace's Receipt Book: Elizabethan Country House Cooking.* London, England: The Salamander Press, 1986.

Frazer, Mrs. *The Practice of Cookery, Pastry, Pickling, Preserving, &c.* Edinburgh: Printed for Peter Hill, Edinburgh, and T. Cadell, London, 1791.

Fries, Adelaide L. *The Road to Salem.* Chapel Hill: The University of North Carolina Press. 1944.

Glasse, Hannah. *First Catch Your Hare: The Art of Cookery Made Plain and Easy, 1747.* A facsimile of the first edition followed by additional recipes from the fifth edition, with a biographical introduction by Tom Jaine, a bibliography and glossary by Alan Davidson and studies of Hannah Glasse's sources and borrowings by Jennifer Stead and Priscilla Bain. Britain: Prospect Books, Allaleigh House, Blackawton, Totnes, TQ9 7DL, 2012.

Hatrak, Amy. *Fanny Pierson Crane: Her Receipts 1796: Confections, Savouries and Drams.* Montclair, New Jersey: Montclair Historical Society, Inc., 1974. Compiled and illustrated by Amy Hatrak, Frances Mills, Elizabeth Shull, Sally Williams.

Hayes, Johnson J. *The Land of Wilkes.* Wilkesboro, North Carolina: Wilkes County Historical Society. 1962.

Washington, Martha. Transcribed by Karen Hess. *Martha Washington's Booke of Cookery and Booke of Sweetmeats,...* New York: Columbia University Press, 1981.

Hooker, Richard J., editor. *A Colonial Plantation Cookbook: The Receipt Book of Harriott Pinckney Horry, 1770.* Columbia, South Carolina: University of South Carolina Press, 1984.

Kitchen Guild of the Tullie Smith House Restoration, ed. *Tullie's Receipts; Nineteenth Century Plantation Plain Style Southern Cooking and Living.* Atlanta, Georgia: Atlanta Historical Society, Inc., 1976.

Kosik, Judith E., editor. *Monroe Family Recipes: Used at Ash Lawn-Highland, Home of James and Elizabeth Monroe.* Charlottesville, Virginia: Ash Lawn-Highland. College of William and Mary. 1988.

Lefler, Hugh T.; William S. Powell. *Colonial North Carolina: A History.* New York: Charles Scribner's Sons. 1973.

McAnulty, Elizabeth Reid, editor, *Camp Cookery; Recipes for Revolutionary War Re-enactors.* 1989.

McMurtry, David Cornelius. *Morgan Bryan (1671-1763), a Danish-Born "Irish Immigrant:"And Some of His Antecedents and Descendants,* compiled by David Cornelius McMurtry, David Randall Bryan, and Kathryn Horton Weiss, Vol 1 of 2, Mil-Mac Publishers. Lexington, Kentucky. 2007.

McMurtry, David C. *Seven Sons and Two Daughters of Morgan Bryan (1671-1763) "Irish Immigrant" and Some of Their Descendants, Vol. II.* Mil-Mac Publishers, Lexington, Kentucky. 2009.

Moss, Kay; Kathryn Hoffman. *The Backcountry Housewife; Vol. I, A Study of Eighteenth-century Foods.* Gastonia, North Carolina: Schiele Museum of Natural History and Planetarium, Inc., 1985.

Pleasures of Colonial Cooking. Newark, New Jersey: Miler-Cory House Museum and the New Jersey Historical Society. 1982.

Preserving the Past; Salem Moravians' Receipts & Rituals. Booneville, North Carolina: An Archival Collection by Carolina Avenue Press, 2003.

Ramsey, Robert W. *Carolina Cradle, Settlement of the Northwest Carolina Frontier, 1747-1762.* Chapel Hill: The University of North Carolina Press. First, December 1964; Second, May 1971; Third, December 1978; Fourth, May 1987.

Randolph, Mary. *The Virginia Housewife or, Methodical Cook: A Facsimile of an Authentic Early American Cookbook.* New York: Dover Publications, 1993.

Raynor, George. *Pioneers and Indians of Back Country North Carolina*; Piedmont Passages: I. Salisbury, North Carolina: Salisbury Post, 1990.

Receipts from the Florida Archives. Tallahassee, Florida.

Roberts, Robert. *The House Servant's Directory.* Boston: Munroe and Francis, 1828.

Sass, Lorna J. *Christmas Feasts.* New York: The Metropolitan Museum of Art, Irena Chalmers Cookbooks, Inc., 1982.

Senseman, L. L. *Receipts.* Salem, North Carolina: Old Salem, Inc. Domestic Skills Program, 1884-1854.

Simmons, Amelia. *The First American Cookbook: A Facsimile of "American Cookery," 1796.* New York: Dover Publications, Inc. 1958.

Smith, Margaret Supplee; Emily Herring Wilson. *North Carolina Women: Making History.* Chapel Hill: The University of North Carolina Press. 1999.

Spencer, Darrell; Virginia R. Weiler; Flora Ann L. Bynum. *The Gardens of Salem: The Landscape History of a Moravian Town in North Carolina.* Winston-Salem, North Carolina: Old Salem, Inc., 1997.

Steed, Jennifer. *Food and Cooking in 18th Century Britain: History and Recipes.* London: Historic Buildings & Monuments Commission for England, 1985.

A Tryon Palace Trifle or Eighteenth Century Cookery, &c. New Bern, North Carolina: Tryon Palace Commission, 1960.

Wall, James W. *History of Davie County in the Forks of the Yadkin.* Spartanburg, South Carolina: The Reprint Company, 1997.

Weiss, Kathryn H. *William Bryan, 1734-1780: Forgotten Friend of Daniel Boone, 1734-1820.* Privately published, 2008.

William Lenoir Papers. Southern Historical Collection, Wilson Library, University of North Carolina at Chapel Hill.

Wigginton, Brooks Eliot. *The Foxfire Book.* Garden City, New York: Doubleday & Company, Inc. 1972.

HISTORIC SITES

Allen Kitchen
Mordecai Historic Park
1 Mimosa Street
Raleigh, NC 27604

Boone Cabin
Whippoorwill Village
11928 NC - 268
Ferguson, NC 28624

Historic Camden Revolutionary
War Site
Kershaw - Cornwallis House
222 Broad Street
Camden, SC 29020

Cleveland House
Wilkes Heritage Museum
100 East Main Street
Wilkesboro, NC 28697

Fort Defiance Historic House
1792 Fort Defiance Drive
Lenoir, NC 28645

Fort Dobbs Historic Site
438 Fort Dobbs Road
Statesville, NC 28625

Hoggatt House
High Point Museum
1859 East Lexington Avenue
High Point, NC 27262

Latta Plantation
5225 Sample Road
Huntersville, NC 28078

Matthews Cabin
Mabry Mill
Blue Ridge Parkway, Milepost 176
Meadows of Dan, VA

Old Salem Visitor Center
900 Old Salem Road
Winston Salem, NC 27101

Pres. James K. Polk State Historic Site
12031 Lancaster Highway
Pineville, NC 28134

Reid Plantation House
Denton Farmpark
1072 Cranford Road
Denton, NC 27239

Savannah Cabin
Foxfire Museum
98 Foxfire Lane
Mountain City, GA 30562

Snow Camp Historic Site
301 Drama Road
Snow Camp, NC 27349

Surry Muster Field
Eastern Trail Head
Overmountain Victory National
Historic Trail
399 NC 268 West
Elkin, NC 28621

Tannenbaum Historic Park
2200 New Garden Road
and
Guilford Courthouse National
Military Park
2332 New Garden Road
Greensboro, NC 27410

Tatum Cabin
Hickory Ridge Living History Museum
591 Horn in the West Drive
Boone, NC 28607

Colonial Williamsburg
Governor's Palace
300 Palace Green Street
Williamsburg, VA 23185